RUCKSACK GUIDE

Mountaineering
in remote areas
of the world

ALUN RICHARDSON

ILLUSTRATED BY GEORGE MANLEY

D0974758

A&C BLACK • LONDON

Note
Whilst every effort has been made to ensure that the content of this book is as technically accurate and as sound as possible, neither the author nor the publishers can accept responsibility for any injury or loss sustained as a result of the use of this material.

Published by A & C Black Publishers Ltd
36 Soho Square, London W1D 3QY
www.acblack.com

First edition 2009

Copyright © 2009 Alun Richardson

ISBN 978 0 7136 8691 3

A CIP catalogue record for this book is available from the British Library.

Acknowledgements
Cover photograph © Alun Richardson
Inside photographs © Alun Richardson
except pp. 46–7, 57 Shutterstock.com and p. 61 Steve Long
Illustrations by © George Manley
Designed by James Watson
Commisioned by Robert Foss
Edited by Lucy Beevor

This book is produced using paper that is made from wood grown in managed, sustainable forests. It is natural, renewable and recyclable. The logging and manufacturing processes conform to the environmental regulations of the country of origin.

Typeset in 9/10pt Din-Light by Margaret Brain, UK

Printed and bound in South China by C&C Offset Printing Co.

The ideas in this book are the culmination of 25 years mountaineering and many hours spent discussing techniques with inspirational mountaineers, rock climbers, Mountain Guides and instructors.

There are many people I need to thank: from my early years with the South Wales Mountaineering Club and the first epics I shared with Alan Dance and Dave Williams, to Steve Lewis and Pat Littlejohn who showed me how to climb harder routes, and the friends and clients I have shared expeditions with.

Special thanks must go to Lesley Jones who supported me through the project and read it many times, Clive Hebblethwaite who chewed over many issues with me in a tent and supplied some photographs, Simon Lowe of Jagged Globe who put the expeditions chapter into shape and Dr Jim Duff who helped with medical issues.

A small army of friends corrected and commented on the text including Matt Spencley, John Biggar and Kit Spencer. I must also thank the following manufacturers, who generously supported the photo shoots: DMM, Lyon Equipment, Mountain Equipment, Face West, Select Solar, Mammut and Fritschi.

Thanks to Rhiannon Richardson and Molly Jones who helped me to sort the text and diagrams; George Manley for his excellent illustrations, and Robert Foss and Lucy Beevor from A&C Black who had the confidence to get behind the book.

Any of the opinions expressed in this book are mine and should not be associated with any of the above people, companies or organisations.

Mountaineering in Remote Areas of the World is the third book in the **Rucksack Guide** series and covers organising small expeditions to remote areas. This handy book can be kept in your rucksack and will help you to gain the experience to climb safely anywhere in the world. The **Rucksack Guide** series tells you *what* to do in a situation, but it does not always explain *why*. If you would like more information behind the decisions in these books, go to *Mountaineering: The Essential Skills for Mountaineers and Climbers* by Alun Richardson (A&C Black, 2008).

Most expeditions to remote parts of the world are lightweight, requiring a small team and minimal equipment. The size and/or remoteness of the mountains mean however that, unlike the Alps, you cannot just turn up and climb – you must research where you are going, organise food, equipment and vaccinations, plan and prepare all logistics, and obtain visas and permits. Much of the information in this book covers organising an expedition to the Himalaya, although it applies to climbing all over the world.

For further information on mountaineering techniques which you would find useful when undertaking small expeditions see *Rock Climbing*, *Winter Mountaineering* and *Alpinism*, all available in the **Rucksack Guide** series.

For more about the author, his photographs and the mountaineering courses he runs go to:
www. alunrichardson.co.uk and
www.freedomphotographs.co.uk.

EXPEDITION STYLES	
Style	Features
Himalayan (conventional) style	Extreme altitude (8000m+) climbs, requiring oxygen use.
	Conducted from a base camp with high camps progressively established using climbers or high-altitude porters.
	Fixed ropes make sections safer and easier for carrying loads.
	Requires large numbers of people and is expensive.
Capsule style (Fig. 1)	Climbers ferry loads to establish a higher camp on the mountain.
	The lower camp is static, providing retreat while another camp is established.
	The process is repeated to a point where the summit can be tackled quickly and lightweight (alpine style).
	Allows acclimatisation on the mountain.

Lightweight alpine style	Alpine climbing without the huts.
	Minimal equipment is carried from base camp for a single ascent to the summit. Acclimatisation is usually done on a smaller peak first.
	No possibility of retreating to a lower camp.
	Planning is easier, requires fewer people, and you can hopefully get up and down before bad weather.
Trekking	'Unsupported', where you carry everything including your food.
	'Assisted', when pack animals or porters carry some or all of your loads.
	You may camp or stay in hostels, huts and teahouses.

Fig. 1 Capsule style on Aconcagua, Argentinian Andes

BEST TIME TO GO

	January	February	March	April	May	June	July	August	September	October	November	December
Best time												
Possible												
Afghanistan/Kyrgyzstan/Pakistan/Tajikistan (Pamirs)												
Alaska												
Algeria/Morocco/Tunisia (Atlas Mountains)												
Antarctica												
Argentina												
Bhutan												
Bolivia												
Canada (Baffin Island)												
Canada (Coast Range)												
Canada (Saint Elias)												

Chile

China/Kazakhstan/ Kyrgyzstan (Tien Shan)

DRC/Uganda (Rwenzori Mountains)

Ethiopia (Simien Mountains)

Greenland

India

Kenya

Mongolia

Nepal

New Guinea (Carstensz Pyramid)

New Zealand

Svalbard

Patagonia

Peru

Tanzania (Mount Kilimanjaro)

Tibet

Note: This does not cover the possibilities for ski mountaineering.

See appendix for more information on where to go. Give yourself enough time – consider the following, which could all impact upon the trip:

- Bad weather, illness, flight delays, bureaucracy
- Organising paperwork, food, visits to agencies
- Time it takes to arrive at the destination country, to travel to the mountain, and to acclimatise.

BUILDING A TEAM
Expeditions can make or break friendships:

- Ensure that everyone agrees upon the objective and how to achieve it.
- Conduct warm-up trips to discover each other's idiosyncracies.
- Be aware of the technical, psychological and physical demands of a remote expedition and how they might affect members.

The size of the team

The style of the expedition and the size of the mountain will dictate the team's size.

- **Larger team** Increases safety, spreads fixed costs, allows a dynamic social mix, but can fragment when sharing equipment, food and tents.
- **A small team of two** Easier to manage and adaptable, but should someone fall ill the whole team must descend. Three or four people will not be much slower and increases safety.

Choosing a leader
All permit-granting bodies in the developing world require a leader. The leader is not necessarily the best climber, but usually has the most experience, and the ability to motivate the group and delegate well.

VISAS, PERMITS AND PERMISSIONS

The Expeditions Commission of the Union International Association Alpinism (UIAA) offers up-to-date information at www.uiaa.ch.

Access to many mountain ranges is governed by regulations. You may need:

- To apply a year ahead for permits, since applications are usually processed through a multitude of government departments (pp. 8–9). Don't leave it too late!
- A national park permit or to pay a conservation fee.
- Special visas, rather than ordinary tourist visas alone.
- To take a liaison officer (LO).
- Permits for two-way radios, filming, helicopter rescue bonds, satellite telephones and guns and ammunition.
- To insure and equip staff.

GETTING THERE

This is often the most expensive part of your trip and the cheapest option is usually not the best; the return flight is fixed, you cannot change passenger's names and it is costly to change dates and times.

Tick	Ensure that:
☐	Your flight ticket has a flexible return date.
☐	You reconfirm your return reservations at least 72 hours before each flight.
☐	You know the baggage allowance for each flight and how to reduce your luggage if necessary.
☐	If you cancel a flight you reclaim the tax and duty paid.
☐	For in-country flights you have a secured seat when you book, because flights into the mountains are often cancelled due to bad weather.

INTERNET CONTACTS

Country/area	Climbing permit required?	Useful websites
Asia		
Afghanistan	Yes	www.afghanconsulate.net
Bhutan	Yes	www.bhutan.gov.bt
China	Maybe	Mountcma@sports.gov.cn
India	Yes	www.indmount.org/index.htm
Kazahkstan	Yes	www.kazakhstan-ecotourism.org
Kyrgyzstan	Yes	www.kac.centralasia.kg
Nepal	Yes	www.nma.com.np and motca@mos.com.np
Pakistan	Yes	www.pakmission-uk.gov.pk
Tibet	Yes	See China
Russia	Yes	www.Mountainguides.ru

The Americas		
Alaska	Yes	www.travelalaska.com
Baffin Island, Canada	Maybe	www.baffinisland.ca
Bolivia, Columbia, Ecuador, Peru, Venezuela	No	www.andes.org.uk
Argentina, Chile, Patagonia	Maybe	www.andes.org.uk
Other		
Antarctica	Yes	www.fco.gov.uk
Greenland	Yes, in the northeast	www.greenlandexpeditionspecialists.com
Russia	Yes	www.Mountainguides.ru

MOUNTAIN ACCESS VIA HELICOPTERS/ PLANES

- Private flights are usually charged hourly to the nearest tenth of an hour. Arrive on time, ready to go.
- Pick up another team or travel part-way by car to reduce costs.
- Beware of baggage allowances on small aeroplanes. Passengers are sometimes weighed.
- Allow enough time to sit and wait for the weather.

PERSONAL AND RESCUE INSURANCE

See www.dh.gov.uk, which states that travellers from the UK to most other European countries, including countries in the former Soviet Union, can get urgent medical treatment, either at reduced cost or – in some cases – for free. If you travel to the US, Canada, the Middle East, Asia, Africa and some other countries you will require private health insurance.

- Whatever reciprocal agreements exist it is essential to have adequate rescue and repatriation insurance.
- Always carry a copy of your insurance policy, and leave another copy with your agent or embassy.
- Have a contingency fund (e.g. credit card) to pay upfront for emergency evacuation.
- Contact your insurance company before any rescue (they may not pay if you have not called them first).
- Does your travel insurance cover everything you need? Baggage may be covered on your house insurance.

Beer talks! Get a large deposit from members to ensure commitment. Consider the following costs:

- Equipment – personal, communal and for staff (porters, LOs etc)
- Transport, both to the country and within the country
- Getting equipment to the country or hiring it
- Hire of porters or pack animals
- Visas, peak fees and permits
- Food, fuel and tips
- Insurance and emergency funds.

Traveller's cheques are often impossible to cash in remote places. Debit/credit cards are charged at official exchange rates that are high, especially in countries with high inflation. Take US dollars to exchange for local currency and several credit cards as back up.

GRANTS [see p. 12]
Most grant-giving bodies require applications well in advance, ask you to provide referees and may even request an interview and a presentation. Do not expect grants to cover the cost of your whole trip.

SPONSORSHIP
Company sponsorship is available if you are willing to work hard, but do not underestimate the difficulties it can bring.

Think about what characteristics of your expedition are most appealing. Offer free advertising, publicity, articles or photographs, but do not offer what you cannot do and, for the sake of other expeditions, if you do offer to do anything, then do it. Meet the company personally. Try to loan equipment, tents etc. from a local outdoor centre or school. Getting media attention increases your chances of sponsorship.

PLANNING

The grand title 'expedition' opens the door for you to gain funding from a wide variety of sources. Most grant-giving bodies will require applications well in advance and do not expect grants to cover the cost of your whole trip.

GRANT-GIVING BODIES	
Grant-giving body	**For**
Alpine Adrian Ashby-Smith Memorial Trust, c/o Mr Jan Ivan-Duke, 39 Sutherland Drive, Newcastle-under-Lyme, Staffordshire ST5 3NZ	Those under 40 years of age who are taking part in their first expedition
Andy Fanshawe Memorial Trust edward.douglas@btinternet.com	Those under 26, lacking funding for an expedition
Augustine Courtauld Trust www.augustinecourtauldtrust.org	Expeditions to the Arctic or Antarctic
British Mountaineering Council www.thebmc.co.uk	Screened at the same time as the MEF (see below). New Peaks, new routes, British firsts or innovative-style ascents.
Captain Scott Society Spirit of Adventure Award and also the Sir Vivian Fuchs Young Adventure Award www.captainscottsociety.co.uk	Expeditions displaying a similar 'spirit of adventure' to Captain Scott and The British Antarctic Expedition of 1910 (young people 11–19 qualify for the second award)
Eagle Ski Club Georgina Travers Award www.eagleskiclub.org.uk	Ski mountaineering expeditions
Edward Wilson Fund http://www.edwardawilson.com /today/	Grants are allocated by the Gino Watkins Memorial Fund committee, particularly applicable to expeditions in which biological and ecological studies are prominent.
Explorers Club Lowell Thomas Award for Scientific Exploration www.explorers.org	Judged on the scientific and practical merits of the expedition
Mount Everest Foundation, MEF www.mef.org.uk	British and New Zealand expeditions proposing mountaineering exploration in high mountain regions

PLANNING

Mount Everest Foundation Alison Chadwick Memorial Grant www.mef.org.uk	To further British and Polish women's mountaineering
Mountaineering Council of Ireland www.mountaineering.ie	Mountaineers living in Ireland
Mountaineering Council of Scotland www.mountaineering-scotland.org.uk	Members must have a strong connection with Scottish mountaineering and an objective of excellence and adventure.
Mugs Stump Award for Climbing www.bdel.com/mugs_stump/	Cutting-edge alpinists exploring new routes in uncharted terrain throughout the world. Only North Americans.
National Geographic Society www.nationalgeographic.com	Exploration and adventure that provides new information about areas either largely or completely unknown, which have great story-telling potential for print and broadcast media. International applicants welcomed.
Nick Estcourt Award www.nickestcourtaward.org/	Expeditions attempting an objective of mountaineering significance
Polartec Challenge www.polartec.com/pulse/challenge.php	To encourage the spirit and practice of outdoor adventure.
Scott Polar Research Institute www.spri.cam.ac.uk	
Ski Club www.skiclub.co.uk	Two grants are available for ski mountaineers in support of exploratory expeditions.
Sports Council for Wales Ground Breaking Expedition Grant Aid www.sports-council-wales.co.uk	The majority of members must be Welsh by birth, parentage or residence in Wales for at least 12 months in the last two years.
Winston Churchill Memorial Trust www.wcmt.org.uk	British citizens only
Wilderness Award www.wildernesslectures.com	An individual undertaking an unusual and exciting project in a wilderness area
Young Explorers' Trust www.theyet.org	Expeditions with most members aged below 20 years old (not usually undergraduate expeditions) involved in discovery and exploration in remote areas

PLANNING

It is common for many expeditions to short circuit the gaining of permits and logistics support by using a commercial company or in-country agent.

ASSISTANCE WITH ORGANISATION	
Type	**Features**
Home commercial companies	• A total expedition package or essential logistical arrangements, including a porter, guide, cook, food tent, sleeping bags, mattresses, transport to and from starting points, flight arrangement, permits, staff insurance etc. • Financial guarantees – they are bound by consumer protection law. • Reassurance that local staff are well looked after. • Intimate knowledge of the mountain range that you are interested in. • No language/cultural barriers if you need to make a complaint.
In-country domestic agents	• Similar service to home commercial companies, but without financial guarantees and UK/US consumer laws. • Leave enough time to speak to them and use an agency that is recommended by friends and/or government-approved.
Doing it yourself	• It doesn't always work out cheaper unless you know exactly what you are doing. • Ensure that you have someone who can speak the language (hire an interpreter).

LEADERSHIP AND GUIDING QUALIFICATIONS

To ensure your safety, employ leaders with an AMGA, IFMGA qualification or MIC award, but also remember that leading an expedition requires skills beyond those assessed on these awards.

● Ask to see their CV and discuss it with them before committing yourself.

● If possible, meet before you go and only employ them if you are confident of their ability to lead.

● Contact the guide's organisation to ensure they can operate legally in the intended country.

● Local guides may know the local mountains intimately, but do not expect the same level of technical climbing support or experience as a qualified guide.

PORTERS AND SHERPAS

Sherpa Common term for anyone who carries (porters) loads or helps on an expedition (strictly the Sherpa are an ethnic group from the most mountainous region of Nepal).

Sirdar Head guide in Nepal Himalaya. Keeps everything running smoothly, organises porters and guides you in the correct direction.

Porter Carries the loads and, in small expeditions, can act as guide and/or cook.

There are three types of porter in India, Pakistan and Nepal:

1 High altitude (expedition) porters: Carry loads from base camp to the summit (Kuli in Nepal).

2 Trekking porters: Carry expedition loads to base camp.

3 General porters (Dhakre in Nepal): Carry the loads/ goods for hotels, stores and the local market.

LIAISON OFFICERS AND INTERPRETERS

Liaison Officers (LOs) are mandatory for climbing some peaks in China, India, Pakistan and Nepal. They are usually a civil servant or army officer (rarely a mountaineer) and won't go above base camp. Regulations for their employment vary.

- Consider them a team member and an asset – if they feel unwanted they can easily create difficulties.
- Ensure you know what equipment you have to provide before you leave.
- Ensure that you provide suitable food – Muslims do not eat pork or pig products, Hindus and Sikhs do not eat beef, and Buddhists and many Hindus are vegetarians.

RECRUITING PORTERS, GUIDES AND COOKS YOURSELF

- When using large numbers of porters, try to distribute employment opportunities and consider using staff from lower villages.
- Always hire in the presence of others and not on the trail.
- Your head guide or Liaison Officer may also be able to help with employment negotiations, or use a domestic agent or commercial company at home.
- Hire recommended porters where possible.
- Large, well-run lodges/guesthouses/hotels/agents can refer you to the best people.
- Hiring staff has other benefits – they look after your camp, help to buy food, help to find accommodation and campsites, cook and show you the best route.

INSURING EMPLOYEES

Independent guides in some countries are registered and sometimes covered by insurance, but this is not always the case. Obtain information at the Porter's Progress offices in Kathmandu and Lukla, the Indian Mountaineering Foundation in India and a government-approved insurer in Pakistan.

Whatever country you are in the welfare of the porters, guides, yak and horsemen are your responsibility whether they are booked through an agency or not:

- Ensure they have clothing and footwear appropriate to season and altitude.
- Some guides/porters may prefer extra money instead of kit, but be absolutely sure that they bring their own clothing and sunglasses.
- Porters at altitude are more at risk from AMS through extra exertion and dehydration. Watch them and carry extra water and food for emergencies. Brief them about symptoms.
- Supply a dedicated shelter, a sleeping pad and a blanket/sleeping bag.
- Provide food and warm drinks, or cooking equipment and fuel.
- Give sick or injured porters the same standard of treatment and rescue facilities as any climber.
- Never send sick/injured porters down alone, even on popular treks, but accompanied by someone who speaks their language and understands their problem. Ensure you have sufficient funds to cover their rescue and treatment.

THE ETHICAL DILEMMA
Portering is a respectable occupation and is essential to rural areas in Nepal, Pakistan and India, where there are few roads in major mountain areas. This exacerbates the problems of poverty and means that you may have to use porters.

Deciding not to use porters because it is 'distasteful' does not solve their poverty. Use them, but treat them well. For further information go to www.ippg.net.

PLANNING

Fig. 2 Using humans to carry equipment is a
necessity for many expeditions, but do we really
need Coca Cola, Pringles and bottled water?

PORTER BACKGROUND
We should be careful not to put all porters
around the world into the same category. For
example, the famous Sherpas of Nepal and Balti
porters of Pakistan still carry loads for a living
outside of expedition work, but porters in
Eastern Africa are impoverished subsistence
farmers who travel from lower elevations in
search of work. The way you recruit porters and
use them should reflect these issues.

ORGANISING PORTERS

During the walks to base camp have a defined stop-off point during the day. Ensure that the final stop is not too late – you won't have easy access to your bag until the porters arrive.

PORTER PAY

National and local governments sometimes have set rates, but they are not easy to enforce when competition is high. Pay a fair rate, judged in terms of local pay (ensure your agent is paying enough).

- If you meet a party on their way out, ask them what rates they paid.
- Underpayment is exploitation, but paying much higher wages may have a destabilising effect on the local economy and may make life difficult for less wealthy expeditions.
- Agree the total price, for each stage or day, including any extras (food, lodging, bad weather days, etc.). Put everything down on paper and get the guide to sign it.
- Give porters a basic allowance for each day of the trek. Negotiate how far they will carry each day and for how many days.

LOAD LIMITS – PORTERS

A good head guide will ensure that porters carry the correct amount. Some countries have legal limits that range between 15–30kg maximum, which can be difficult to enforce. A difficult issue arises when there is a shortage of porters or young, fit porters want to carry double loads to maximise their earnings. Common sense should prevail! Any load carried may need to be adjusted for:

● The porter's personal kit and food
● The difficulty and duration of the trek
● Altitude, trail and weather conditions
● The contents of the pack (sleeping bags are much lighter than steel cutlery!)
● The porter's age, gender and physical ability.

PORTER LOAD LIMITS		
Load criteria for popular destinations		
	Employment criteria	*Weight (including personal allowance)*
Nepal	Judged fit to work by physical appearance alone	Above 4000m (13,123ft): 25kg (55lb) Below 4000m (13,123ft): 30kg (66lb)
Peru	Must produce a certificate from the Ministry of Health to work	Adult male: 25kg (55lb) Adult female or adolescent: 20kg (44lb)
Tanzania	Climbing experience	25kg (55lb)

PLANNING

EXPERT TIP

Kit Spencer
summitreck@trekking.
wlink.co.np

'Be ruthless in reducing the amount of gear you take. Freight and excess baggage charges are steep. Import duties can hurt, and once in the country you still have to move it to the mountain. Round barrels are difficult for both porters and yaks. Square barrels take up less space and are easier to carry.'

Fig. 3 *Porters may be used to carrying heavy loads, but that does not mean they don't require care – ensure loads are well packed.*

Fig. 4 Weighing stations for loads are few-and-far-between and ground agencies often find their way around the law.

Packing porter loads

Some porters may be experienced at carrying heavy loads, but you must ensure they are packed carefully for security of the load and the porter's welfare.

- Keep the load against the carrier's back, free from sharp corners and edges. Ensure that paraffin/petrol containers do not leak.

- Keep loads secure from theft – a good porter will not resent this, as it puts him beyond suspicion should something go missing.

- Number the loads and keep a list of the porters' names against load numbers and contents, or give porters tickets/tags with the load number.

- Pack sufficient food for the route to avoid disturbing loads en route.

Tipping

Decide what the tip will be from the start, making it clear that tips are for good service and not guaranteed; a bonus system could be organised beforehand with the agency. The amount varies, but in Nepal, India and Pakistan it is usually around 10 per cent of the fee and is often distributed during a celebratory dinner. Tips for guides and cooks are usually treated separately. Ensure that the tips are distributed fairly, and don't forget porters that leave the expedition early!

Most importantly, ensure that the promise of a tip does not encourage porters to carry more than necessary or undertake unsafe tasks. Do not pay bonuses to high altitude porters based on them getting to the summit.

Fig. 5 *Our head guide in Africa receives a tip for excellent service.*

LOAD LIMITS – PACK ANIMALS

Animal	Load
Mules and horses	Up to 60kg
Yaks	40–50kg (less in spring)
Donkeys (burros)	Up to 40kg
Llamas	Up to 30kg
A team of ten sled dogs	Up to 300kg in soft snow

You may find the way pack animals are treated disturbing, but there are things you can do:

- Pack your equipment carefully and keep sharp edges padded (round barrels are difficult to carry).
- Ensure the animal has a saddle blanket to reduce sores and padding and keep the load off the spine.
- Ensure the load is evenly balanced.
- Ensure enough animal food is carried.
- Refuse to use an animal that looks sick.

Fig. 6 *Pack animals do not necessarily cover greater distances.*

COPING WITH A DIFFERENT CULTURE

Adjusting to a different country and encountering poverty can be difficult.

● Read about the country's history, society, political structure, environment, art and religion.

● Develop basic language skills to improve the quality of communication and show respect: forms of greeting, please and thank you, days of the week, time and numbers.

● Acquaint yourself with socially acceptable ways of doing things/gestures (giving the OK sign, shaking hands, or eating with your left hand can be offensive in some countries).

● Avoid displaying bare skin in public places (even non-Muslim countries) where it is unacceptable for religious or social reasons.

● Dress conservatively in developing countries and male-dominated societies. Women should cover their arms, legs and cleavage (and their hair in Muslim countries). See www.Journeywoman.com for more information.

● Be careful of making eye contact or smiling – in some cultures it may suggest that you want a person's company.

● Women might like to wear dark glasses, wear a wedding ring or carry photos of their husband and children (whether real or not).

BARTERING

Bartering does not make you a scrooge – traders think you are stupid if you do not, and it is expected in many countries. Only bargain if you intend to buy and always have a fair figure in mind.

BEGGING

- Do not hand money to individuals or give sweets (which rot teeth), pens and paper (which can be sold) to children – you are perpetuating the problem and possibly undermining the parents' authority. Instead, buy locally made goods, services and food to help.

- Developing countries are often corrupt – charities, such as Oxfam and Comic Relief, are highly trained and experienced in getting money and resources to the right people.

TAKING PHOTOGRAPHS

- Being on an expedition does not automatically give you the right to photograph anything.

- Do not intrude on private ceremonies; ask first and spend time sitting with the locals to gain their trust before you snap them.

- Don't pay children to take photographs, as they are encouraged to beg and miss school.

- Proceed with caution when taking photos of bridges, official buildings, people in uniform, aeroplanes and airports, or religious buildings and ceremonies – your film may be confiscated.

Fig. 7 *Showing locals the shots on the digital camera. If you promise to send the photos, please do it.*

Do not worry too much about tropical illnesses – the most likely source of medical problem is a road accident, however you also need to protect yourself from crime.

FAKE POLICE
Be suspicious of anyone asking to see your money or ID. Check their documents or request to be taken to the nearest police station.

THIEVES
Don't be ostentatious with your property or cash. Be suspicious if somebody slows you down (even falling over) and especially if the same person is behind you for a few minutes. Use a decoy wallet and spread money around your luggage and person. Avoid carrying lots of luggage – the bigger the luggage, the more visible you are. Using an accomplice, often women and children, to distract you is a common pick-pocket's method. Don't try to apprehend them unless there are police near by.

FOOD/DRINK
Take care when accepting food or drink on a bus/ train/etc. – it may be drugged.

MONEY CHANGERS
Do not exchange money on the black market – it may be switched with worthless notes.

PUBLIC TRANSPORT
Crowded public transport is a thief's paradise. Be wary of taxis you hail on the street. Call a reputable taxi service recommended by your hotel.

RENTING CARS

Carry a mobile phone and an emergency number. Never pick up hitchhikers. Never get out of your car if another vehicle bumps into it – wait for the police to arrive.

WHEN DRIVING

Keep your luggage hidden and windows closed, especially at traffic lights in busy towns. Do not rely on public telephones. Use the car boot for luggage.

ACCOMMODATION

Choose carefully, arrive in daylight and ask to see the room before accepting it. Check that the door locks properly (consider carrying a rubber door stop or a rape alarm to tape across the door) and that your room number and location is kept private. Avoid ground floor rooms or any that have easy access from outside. Do not get in an elevator unless you feel completely safe.

Fig. 8 *Beware of crime in busy towns (Delhi, India).*

MEDICAL PREPARATION

Before leaving home:

- Visit your doctor and obtain spares of any medications you regularly take. Inform the rest of the team that you are taking medication.
- Discuss the risks and medication with a well-informed doctor.
- Have a dental check-up at least three months before departure.
- Depart healty: eat probiotic yoghurt regularly before you go for well-balanced gut flora.

IMMUNISATION

Check that you are properly vaccinated against polio, tetanus, typhoid and hepatitis and take advice on other potential illnesses, including the risks of malaria, depending on your itinerary. Yellow fever is still required for parts of Africa, South America and Asia. You might not be allowed to fly without a certificate of vaccination (beware of crossing borders).

Vaccinations take time to become fully effective, so consult your doctor at least eight weeks before departure. See www.nhs.co.uk for information.

FIRST AID

Do not expect rescue or help. Serious medical mishaps are rare, however:

- Watch each other for signs of illness. Look for 'grumble, mumble, stumble, tumble' (Dr Jim Duff).
- All team members should have a basic knowledge of crisis management.
- Each member should carry a small personal first aid kit, in addition to a more substantial expedition kit, and know how to use it.
- Carry a first aid manual such as *First Aid and Wilderness Medicine* (Dr Jim Duff, 2001).
- Go to www.treksafe.com for further medical advice.

GLASSES AND CONTACT LENSES

Contact lenses can be used successfully, but as everyone is constrained to wear sunglasses once above the snowline, it is easier to wear sunglasses with prescription lenses. Opticians regularly make them, but it is not always easy to get a pair suitable for mountaineering, i.e. those that have been designed to ensure little light enters from the sides, bottom or around the nose.

Close-fitting, wrap-around style glasses are common, but these don't always come with the option of taking prescription lenses. The easiest and most cost-effective solution is to buy standard mountaineering sunglasses from an outdoor shop and then to have them re-glazed by an optician with prescription lenses, darkened with your referred tint, and other lens coatings, such as extra UV filters.

REMOTE EXPEDITION FIRST AID CHECKLIST

Tick	Medicine	For
☐	Roll of zinc oxide tape	Covering blisters, taping injuries and dressings
☐	Paracetamol/ Ibuprofen	Simple analgesia, musculoskeletal injuries and altitude headaches
☐	Tincture of iodine	Purifying water and antiseptic
☐	Gauze dressing	Simple wound dressings
☐	Compeed or similar dressing	Padding for nasty blisters
☐	Cling film	Useful for absolutely everything
☐	Roll of duct tape	Covering blisters (zinc oxide rucks up)

The remainder of the kit really depends on how far from help you are:

☐	Stronger painkillers (morphine/tramadol/penthrox)	Stronger pain relief. Discuss with a doctor who will give you training on administration and advice on customs clearance.
☐	Strong anti-inflammatories	Reducing inflammation
☐	Sam Splints/Kendrick Traction Device	Immobilising a fracture. A KTD reduces internal bleeding and shock.
☐	Antibiotics (co-amoxiclav /ciprofloxacin/ metronidazole/ flucloxacillin)	A wide variety of infections, from dental abscess to diarrhoea
☐	Lotions (antifungal, antihistamine, steroid, antibiotic, Clotrimazole, Anthisan, 1 per cent hydrocortisone, Fucidin, antiseptic spray or liquid)	Irritating skin conditions
☐	Potions (Dexamethasone, Nifedipine, Acetazolamide, oxygen and a PHC).	Altitude expeditions where there is a risk of AMS, HACE and HAPE
☐	Crepe bandages/ steristrips/sutures/ super glue	Dressings and wound closure

You are often days away from a hospital and medical treatment, so come prepared.

See *Rucksack Guide: Alpinism* for guidance on acclimatisation and Acute Mountain Sickness (AMS). The more serious altitude illnesses of High Altitude Pulmonary Oedema (HAPE) and High Altitude Cerebral Oedema (HACE) occur more frequently above 3500m, brought on by ascending too rapidly. HAPE is twice as common as HACE and is more likely to kill. They may occur together, so if you find one, check for the other. If you feel unwell at altitude, it is altitude illness until proven otherwise.

HAPE

The leakage of fluid into and around the lungs reduces your ability to absorb oxygen. Respiratory infections increase the risk and HAPE is antagonised by cold temperatures and exercise. AMS can precede HAPE, but does occur alone.

POSSIBLE SYMPTOMS

- Loss of energy/tiredness.
- More than usual breathlessness.
- A cough that may start off dry, becoming bubbly and wet with frothy sputum, which may be blood-stained once the illness is advanced.
- There may be a mild fever, making it difficult to distinguish from pneumonia (infection of the lungs), which has sometimes led to fatal misdiagnosis.
- Rate of breathing (breaths per minute) and heart rate rise disproportionately at rest.
- May hear crackles in the lung fields with a stethoscope once the disease is advanced.
- The lips and nail beds take on a bluish tinge (cyanosis), because the fluid in the lungs prevents oxygen getting into the blood. This can lead to unconsciousness.

TREATMENT

- If available, give oxygen immediately, either from a bottle or by using a portable hyperbaric chamber (remember that descent is the definitive treatment – do not delay, even after the patient has recovered sufficiently).

- Minimise exertion, which worsens HAPE – carry the patient (they may need to be sitting or propped up), assist them or at least carry their pack.

- Keep the patient warm and hydrated and give them food or a sugary drink.

- The drug nifedipine is used to prevent recurrence during descent.

HACE

The end-stage of AMS. It can develop very quickly. Death is due to the accumulation of fluid in and around the brain, which increases the pressure within the skull.

Whilst AMS and HACE may be linked, don't expect casualties to necessarily exhibit mild symptoms of AMS before presenting with clear symptoms of HACE (or HAPE). Depending on the rate of ascent and any one person's ability to acclimatise, symptoms of HACE and HAPE can present very quickly, e.g. in someone who only the evening before appeared quite well.

POSSIBLE SYMPTOMS

- Severe headache and vomiting, but absence of a headache must not be taken as absence of HACE. (If someone is hallucinating near the summit of Kilimanjaro then, headache or not, they are one symptom short of near death).

- Lack of physical coordination (clumsy hands and unsteady feet) and, as the condition progresses, they may not be able to walk at all, and will stagger or fall when asked to stand upright (especially when they close their eyes).

- Mental symptoms – any or all of the following: confusion, disorientation, irrationality, unusual quietness or noisiness, hallucinations.
- Eventual sleepiness and lethargy before slipping into coma and dying.

TREATMENT
- If available, give oxygen immediately either from a bottle or by using a portable hyperbaric chamber (but remember that descent is the definitive treatment – do not delay, even after the patient has recovered sufficiently).
- Administer dexamethasone regularly.
- Carry the patient or assist to descend.
- Clumsiness can persist for days, even weeks, despite the patient's apparent recovery.

ABOVE 7000M
Even when fully acclimatised, avoid spending more than three or four days above 7000m, because you will experience weight loss, worsening appetite, poor sleep, increasing apathy and minor ailments such as a viral sore throat or chest infection. At extreme altitude, site the base camp at or below 5000m, so that proper recovery can take place between sorties to higher elevations.

USING DIAMOX
AMS is best-prevented by sensible acclimatisation, but you can use Diamox (acetazolamide) to make the process of acclimatisation more comfortable or to minimise the symptoms of AMS. Its use should definitely be considered in any forced rapid ascent. It increases your rate of breathing, thereby improving oxygenation during sleep. Side effects include an

increased need to pass water, tingling in the fingers and toes, and making carbonated drinks taste flat. It has not been shown to have an effect above 7000m.

Half of one tablet (125mg) should be taken twice daily as a trial at home for two days, several weeks before a visit to altitude. Assuming no unpleasant side effects are experienced, take the drug in the same dose for three days before staying at 3500m and thereafter for two or three days until you feel acclimatised, for about five days in all.

Acetazolamide is a sulfonamide medication, and persons severely allergic to sulfa medicines should not take it.

WARNING!

Sleeping pills can be dangerous and predispose you to altitude sickness, because they depress your respiration, reducing your oxygen uptake. Melatonin is a sleep aid that has no contraindications at altitude. Use an inflatable mattress, stay warm and relax.

THE PILL AT ALTITUDE

Combined oral contraceptives do not affect acclimatisation, but there is a theoretical risk of blood clots. If you are to spend more than one week higher than 4500m you should discuss the risks of continuing to take the oral contraceptive with a doctor.

A PAC won't cure the casualty, but it may ensure he can descend more quickly to safety. Used correctly at 6000m, the pressure inside can be increased to an equivalent altitude of 3250m (put an altimeter inside).

● Include a sleeping bag, vomit bag, water bottle and pillow with the patient, and maintain eye contact during treatment.

● Carefully add oxygen only if the bag cannot subsequently take someone down to below the height at which the patient was last well.

● As pressure increases, warn the patient to equalise their ears (put an altimeter inside).

● Patients with breathing difficulties may need to have the head end of the bag elevated and unconscious patients should be propped on to their side.

● Treatment time varies and should be judged by the patient's response.

● Reduce the pressure slowly. Open the zip gradually when the side of the bag starts to collapse.

● Once removed from the bag, HACE or HAPE may 'rebound'. It is unpredictable, but be ready to restart treatment at any time.

EXPERT TIP

Dr Jim Duff
www.treksafe.com.au

'If someone is very ill at altitude and you can't figure out why, the patient should be re-warmed, rehydrated, re-sugared and re-oxygenated (through either descent, bottled or hyperbaric means).'

Fig. 9 Igor Gamow designed the first commercial PAC in the late 1980s.

High altitude can also lead to the following conditions:

Retinal haemorrhages Descend if vision is interfered with.

Snow blindness Very painful and serious.

Sleeplessness Lying for eight hours at rest with a relaxed mind and body is supposedly the equivalent of six hours sleep.

Weight loss On a three to six week expedition to altitudes over 3600m expect to lose 5.5–7.5kg.

Dehydration Lowered oxygen levels and AMS stimulate urine flow. Drink just enough to keep your urine pale and plentiful.

Sunburn/windburn Prepare for increased UV, the cold and the wind.

Peripheral oedema (swelling of hands and feet) Symptoms usually diminish after a few days, and they are not an indication of HACE or HAPE.

TRAVELLER'S DIARRHOEA

Diarrhoea is common, but not every loose movement is serious. It is most commonly contracted through contaminated food and water, so avoid the following:

- Untreated water and ice cubes
- Chang (rice beer, usually made with untreated water)
- Raw vegetables and salad
- Uncooked or rare-cooked fish and meat
- Unpeeled fruit
- Fresh fruit juice
- Cheese
- Ice cream.

With the onset of diarrhoea, use oral rehydration solution. Use anti-diarrhoea agents, such as Imodium or Lomotil, sparingly. If diarrhoea persists, antibiotics may be necessary.

DIARRHOEA TREATMENT

Type of infection	Symptoms	Treatment
Bacterial (10 x more common)	● Watery diarrhoea ● Rotten egg burps	Ciprofloxacin (500mg, twice a day for three days)
Protozoal (giardia, amoeba)	● Takes at least a week to develop and comes on slowly ● Rotten egg burps	Metronidazole (800mg, three times a day for four days)

Note: The above drugs should not be given to children and pregnant women.

KHUMBU COUGH
A persistent, non-serious dry cough caused by the cold and very dry air at altitude. Make repeated examinations for more serious problems, such as HAPE. Use a scarf or mask to warm and humidify the air.

HEARTBURN
Very common at altitude, probably because the tannin in tea, which is consumed in large amounts, is abrasive and irritating to the stomach. Also a side-effect of acclimatisation to altitude. Drink more herbal tea and take antacids.

TOOTHACHE
Toothach can end an expedition and visiting a village dentist is frightening. Take care when eating hard things, like popcorn, and beware of small stones in local rice. Try paracetamol or ibuprofen (do not rub into the gums) and antibiotics if swelling or fever occurs (erythromycin for those allergic to penicillin). Antiseptics containing benzocaine applied directly to the tooth and gum temporarily relieve pain. Carry a temporary filling kit.

COLDS AND SORE THROATS
- Pay scrupulous attention to hand washing/drying or use alcohol gel (wipes are not adequate) to reduce the spread of infection.
- The majority of respiratory tract infections are viral and antibiotics have no affect.
- An obvious sign of bacterial infection is a foul-smelling breath on exhalation or coughing up of discoloured sputum, either yellow or green or rusty coloured; this suggests infection.
- If sputum is coming up from the lungs, assume this is HAPE, and treat with immediate descent.
- Travellers to countries experiencing outbreaks of avian influenza should avoid areas with live poultry.

HEAT EXHAUSTION AND HEAT STROKE
Heat exhaustion The result of salt and water loss through sweating and not drinking enough. Symptoms are profuse sweating, dizziness, and fatigue.

Heat stroke Can be fatal and differs from heat exhaustion in that the body temperature rises above 40°C; sweating may cease; the body will be very hot to touch; and headache is likely, as is mental disturbance. Urgent treatment is needed. Get out of the sun, fan the patient, give water and cool the body with cool liquid, or even snow or ice, followed by evacuation to hospital.

WOMEN'S ISSUES
- Occasionally women stop menstruating or their cycle becomes irregular when travelling for a long time. If in doubt, get a pregnancy test.
- Tampons and sanitary towels are unobtainable in parts of Africa, Asia and South America.
- Yeast infections are likely to recur in warm, moist climates. Wearing loose-fitting cotton underwear and skirts rather than pants may help.
- Drink lots of water to reduce the risk of cystitis.

PANIC ATTACKS, ANXIETY AND DEPRESSION

Expedition life isn't for everyone. The technical, psychological and physical demands of an expedition can be difficult to cope with, and anxiety and poor sleep are common. Lack of privacy and isolation from home can change people's moods daily. Fear of the unknown and worrying about the climb can induce acute panic attacks. The breathlessness, headaches and dizziness caused by panic attacks can resemble AMS.

All team members should look for changes in moods and be encouraging and supportive while excluding physical problems. It is worth using the buddy system, where you pair off to sleep and look after each other, at altitude. In my experience admitting that everyone is apprehensive, tired, fed up, cold or nauseous helps tremendously! Descending to base camp or lower can be a great help, but if the problems persist then a return home may be in order.

Fig. 10 Recognise when someone is having a rough day, when they need support or when all they need is space.

INSECTS AND OTHER SMALL CREATURES

It is rare to be bitten on an expedition by something that can kill you directly (thanks to bugbog.com for information).

VENOMOUS
- Insects sting as a form of defence.
- Stings are painful, red and swell up to 30cm around the sting site.
- In sensitive individuals a whole body reaction (anaphylactic shock) can occur, with redness, hives (itchy raised skin lumps) and swelling far away from the sting site.
- Systemic reactions can be life threatening – those with a known allergy to stings should carry an emergency syringe with 0.1 per cent adrenaline and know how to use it.

NON-VENOMOUS
- Insects bite to feed on your blood.
- Not generally dangerous, because allergic reactions are rare.
- For most of us the bites just cause itching. However, they do spread diseases like malaria, yellow fever, Lyme disease, typhus and encephalitis.

Ticks
Small blood-feeding parasites often found in tall grass and shrubs all year-round. There are hundreds of species carrying many diseases including Lyme disease, Rocky Mountain Spotted Fever and encephalitis. While tick bites are common and serious illnesses are rare, a circle of pink skin around the bite may indicate infection.

Ticks crawl around for hours before latching on, and then feed for days. When fully engorged, the tick will drop off leaving behind saliva, toxin and possible infection.

- Keep covered in tick-infested areas and search for ticks daily.

- Ticks cause itchiness, because their small bodies protrude from the skin.

- If removed early, they have very little effect. Take them off with fine tweezers or a noose of dental floss while avoiding squeezing the body, or use insect repellent.

- If the head is left behind, cut it out, otherwise infection and poisoning may occur.

Leeches (Fig. 11)

Blood-sucking worm-like creatures common in wet warm areas (monsoon seasons), especially jungles and rainforests. Leeches don't carry disease, but can cause secondary infections if they are not carefully removed. To detach a leech, gently pull it off, allow it to bleed, inspect your skin for remaining mouth parts and then apply antiseptic. Cover the area for several days to prevent scratching (the cause of most infections). Insect repellent also removes leeches and ticks from your skin without the risk of separating them from their mouth parts.

Fig. 11 *Insect repellent is the cleanest means of removal.*

Malaria kills two million people every year. It is not a problem above 2000m, because the malarial parasite cannot survive. If you are below 2000m for any length of time you should take precautions, even if you stop in an airport for several hours.

- Do not rely on anti-malarial drugs alone – try to avoid being bitten.
- Wear long-sleeved shirts tucked into your trousers, and trousers into socks, especially in the evenings and at night.
- Apply repellents to clothing, shoes, tents, mosquito nets and other gear.
- If you decide to chance passing quickly through a malarial area en route, carry a course of treatment, as developing malaria on a mountain could be fatal.
- Discuss your needs and potential anti-malarial side-effects with an experienced doctor.

Fig. 12 A mosquito sucking blood

Fig. 13 *Mosquitoes thrive in warm and moist areas, such as the Amazon Basin.*

INSECT REPELLENT

- **Deet (Diethyl-toluamide)** Very effective, but it is not kind to skin, and possibly affects nylon and plastic, so only use it on clothes or nets. Check with your doctor before use, especially if pregnant.
- **Mosiguard** Relatively natural (citrodiol and eucalyptus) and often effective, so save Deet for the heavy duty mosquito attacks.
- **NeemCare Herbal Insect Repellent** Burned in India to repel insects. Has successfully repelled the voracious midges that plague the Scottish Highlands, as well as mosquitoes.

POST-EXPEDITION

If you suffer fever or flu-like illness up to one year after travel, inform your doctor of the possibility of malaria.

Only two species of snake are very dangerous: adders and vipers. Poisonous adders have short, stiff fangs. This group includes Cobras in Asia, Mambas in Africa, Tiger and Coral snakes in the Americas, most breeds of Australian snake and sea serpents. You are unlikely to come across snakes at altitude or when the ground is continually frozen, but you may when approaching lower altitude mountains or walking in the foothills.

- Very few snake bites are accidental; like most animals, snakes only attack if threatened or surprised.
- If a snake is within striking distance, stay still and move back very slowly. Snakes are very quick and may strike in defence at any sudden movement.
- Snakes on the ground hardly ever bite higher than 30cm so wear stout boots and long, tough trousers or gaiters.
- Check either side of your tread when walking in snake territory.
- Many snakes are nocturnal, so take a torch.
- If you are bitten and the snake can be safely killed, bring it into hospital with the victim.
- In Australia, do not clean wounds unless the snake has been firmly identified.
- Be careful with snake charmers – although the snake's fangs are removed, they re-grow them and they can still be venomous.

TREATING A SNAKE BITE

1   Calm the victim and lay them down to slow the spread of venom.

2   Allow the bite to bleed freely for 30 seconds.

3   In Australia, apply a compression bandage to the whole limb, tight enough to wriggle two fingers under it.
    Elsewhere, do not apply a compression bandage unless you are many hours from medical help and life-threatening symptoms start to develop (i.e. breathing difficulties).

4   Remove any jewellery or tight-fitting clothing.

5   Immobilise/splint the bitten limb and keep it at heart level (gravity-neutral). Holding it too high causes venom to travel to the heart, but holding it too low causes more swelling.

6   Do not administer any medicine, alcohol or food.

7   Get the victim to hospital, with minimum exertion on the part of the victim.

8   If you have to nurse the victim without medical help follow the advice above, maintain hydration and be prepared to give CPR.

USING SUCTION

If the hospital is more than three hours away and the snake is deadly, it may be acceptable to cut and suck or use suction. A suction device can help to draw the venom out of the wound in the first 5–10 minutes without making cuts. This is not usually recommended – the cut may cause secondary infection and increase blood flow, which may accelerate the flow of venom to the heart. However, if required:

- Wrap a light bandage above and below the wound, clean the area with antiseptic and clean every few minutes.
- Make cuts with a short, sharp blade near the bite site and start to suck.
- Follow steps 5–8 last of the snake bite procedure.

If used properly, a suction device can actually remove up to 30 per cent of the venom.

ANTI-VENOM

Snake specific anti-venom, when available, should only be administered by those experienced in its use. It is impractical in remote regions because it must be refrigerated.

SPIDER BITES

There are only several species in Australia and South America that are really dangerous.

- Take care at night as spiders are mainly nocturnal; check and shake out clothes and shoes.
- In high risk areas, keep bedding off the floor and walls, restricting access to just the supports. Check bedding and bags before getting in.

- Bites from the truly poisonous spiders, such as Funnel Webs, should be treated like snakebites – seek medical assistance as soon as possible.

- If you are bitten, try to kill the insect for identification purposes – don't panic, as very few people die of a spider bite.

- Apply ice to the bite site and treat symptoms with antihistamines and painkillers.

DOG BITES

Carry a big stick in towns and cities and use it. Apart from the obvious injuries, a bite can spread infections like tetanus or rabies. Everyone should be adequately covered for tetanus before leaving home, but rabies is more of a problem. If you are bitten:

- Clean the wound with soap or detergent and running water for 30 minutes.

- Apply antiseptic such as iodine, chlorhexidine or alcohol.

- If you suspect the animal has rabies, or it is common in the area, seek medical assistance immediately.

- Immunisation should be administered within 24–48 hours, and rabies immunoglobulin infiltrated around the wound. Vaccination within days of exposure is 100 per cent effective in preventing the progression of the infection to encephalitis. If you have been immunised against rabies prior to being bitten, you will still require further doses of vaccine.

With the exception of polar bears, larger carnivores are not known to attack parties of four or more people.

TYPES OF BEAR

Bear	Habitat	Notable characteristics
Polar bear	Sea ice in the Arctic Circle, from which they hunt seals (in several areas they appear on land, usually on beaches or in bear corridors between beaches).	Agile on rough terrain and excellent swimmers. Curious, and investigate any strange object, smell or noise. They are programmed to kill!
Brown or grizzly bear	Found in the north-west and Alaska in the US and in Alberta, British Columbia, the Yukon and the Northwest Territories in Canada.	Big enough to kill a man with a single swipe of its paw. Tend to attack humans only if startled or with young.
Black bear	Found in 41 of the 50 US states, all Canadian provinces (but not Prince Edward Island) and parts of Mexico. Also in the forests of Asia.	Smaller relative of the brown bear. Rarely attack humans, but will if starving.

There is no 100 per cent defence from a bear attack – avoidance is best. There are broadly two kinds of attack:

1) Defence The bear shows anger, but simply wants you removed as a threat, and not to kill you. If you surprise or upset a mother with cubs it will attack to protect them.

2) Hunger Starving bears are particularly dangerous – they may stalk you without anger symptoms, but their intent is deadly. Avoid areas where bears feed such as fruit groves and streams with fish.

AVOIDING ATTACK

- Arrange the tents in lines or semi-circles so that you have a free view of approaching bears at a distance of at least 200m.
- Place all 'smelly' areas downwind from the sleeping area and do not bring food or anything strong-smelling into your tent.
- Pack food in airtight containers and store 20m from your campsite.
- Do not trek alone, and make noise when on the move so the bear is not surprised by you.
- Bears standing on their hind legs are curious rather than planning on lunch, so be cool and slowly back off.

WHAT TO DO IF A BEAR ATTACKS

- If a bear approaches slowly, experts suggest talking calmly and firmly, then backing away.
- Do not make eye contact or threaten it, and it may lose interest. If this doesn't work, be aggressive, make a noise and wave your hands.

If a bear does run at you on its hind legs making unpleasant noises including puffing, teeth chomping and snarling, then consider the following:

- It may be a 'bluff' charge, which is not uncommon. The bear will veer off or stop at the last moment if you stay still (slowly back away).

- Running may trigger a chase response from an animal that would otherwise not bother. Run for safety **only** if you are sure you can reach it before the bear!

- Trees are not a good refuge. Black and brown bears climb them all day and older grizzlies are proficient tree shakers.

- Water is equally useless. Brown and polar bears are excellent swimmers and will not get hypothermia or drown (unlike you).

- Spray repellent 'pepper' spray in the bear's face, which irritates its eyes and lungs. There are reports of these sprays saving lives!

- Fight back. This may work with a black bear, but don't try it with a polar or a grizzly bear unless you have a weapon.

WHEN A GRIZZLY OR POLAR BEAR ATTACKS

Roll up into a ball, protect vital organs and pretend to be dead. Bears who do not want to eat you may roll around on you for a bit, or just go away. Black bears are not as aggressive as grizzlies and will usually run away if you surprise them, so try to escape or scare the bear away.

SHOOTING A POLAR BEAR

- Polar bears can duck under flares. One member should use the flare and another should be ready with the gun.

- Shooting a polar bear is a criminal offence if you haven't tried to scare it off first. The decision to shoot a polar bear is a personal one, but make it quickly! The shotgun should be 15 calibres and not greased. Carry it with you at all times and test fire it occasionally.

- Wait until the bear is within 10–15m before shooting. The first shot is the most important one. Kneel down; if the bear is broadside aim for the low neck area, if the bear is facing you aim for the low, centre neck between the shoulders.

Fig 14 Only Greenland residents who are full-time hunters are allowed to hunt polar bears. Report all catches, including struck-and-lost polar bears, to the relevant authorities.

Never walk closer than 100m to wild animals, and never feed a wild animal because it will learn to associate humans with food (it also make them ill).

COMMON WILD ANIMALS

Yaks	• You are more likely to encounter a yak-cow crossbreed (dzopkyo), rather than true yaks, which have less stamina, are more irritable, and are uncomfortable at low altitudes.
	• Stay clear of the front horns and the back end and, when passing, stay on the uphill side of yaks.
	• Never use yaks to carry a casualty.
Sled dogs	• Bred to attack polar bears, so never approach them without their handler (the alpha male of the pack).
	• If you must approach, act like an alpha male and kick them if they come close; they may want to test their dominance by fighting with you.
Wolves/foxes	• Only dangerous to humans if they are trapped, threatened or carry rabies.
Water buffalo	• Rogue male buffalos that have left the herd are among the most dangerous animals you can encounter and are known to charge without warning.
	• Ensure you are accompanied and walk close to an armed ranger.

Yak, Zanskar Valley,
Ladakh, India

A plan of action is essential – imagine how you would like to cope in a crisis.

- Stay calm and assess the situation slowly and methodically.
- Avoid rash decisions with incomplete information.
- Establish a plan to resolve the situation quickly and efficiently. Do not forget the rest of the team.
- Never hesitate to bring out the emergency equipment, put up a tent or get some warm food in time.

MEDICAL EMERGENCIES

Carry a Salbutamol inhaler, an assortment of syringes and needles, treatment for anaphylaxis (adrenaline), Piriton and hydrocortisone. Know how to give an enema and practice it.

WHEN TO EVACUATE QUICKLY

Several injuries in remote places require rapid evacuation and help must be called immediately, by radio or phone, or by sending messages (send to no less than two people).

Head injury

Can result in uncontrolled swelling of the brain. The duration of unconsciousness tells you roughly the severity of injury, though if bleeding occurs inside the skull, a patient may recover well then fall unconscious some time later.

If a person has been unconscious for more than 5–10 minutes, has significant facial trauma, a severe headache that gets worse, altered mental status, deteriorating level of consciousness or uncontrolled ongoing nausea and vomiting, evacuate.

Spinal injury

Can result in significant localised pain or tenderness of the neck or back – it is an unstable injury until proven otherwise. Keep the victim still and gently move into a neutral position (flat with the arms by the sides and the legs straight) once a primary survey is completed. If they are unconscious and/or vomiting turn them on their side using a log roll. If evacuation has to be made without medical help, splint the victim's back and neck, place them on a stretcher and keep it horizontal.

Open fractures

The bone penetrates the skin, exposing it to contamination. Place pressure to keep the bone ends clean, splinting any gross deformity.

SIGNALLING FOR HELP

All shiny material can act as signal mirrors, and flashing lights always attract attention. Distress signals should be at least 3m high, visible and in contrast with the background. If you can, make a fire, or if you have flares or signal rockets use them, but only when you hear a helicopter or plane.

SIGNALLING TO A HELICOPTER

Stand with both arms raised in a 'Y', meaning 'yes'. A person with only one arm raised and one arm straight down means that all is well; imitating an 'N', meaning 'no'. Other conventional distress signals are six whistling signals (you can blow a whistle for much longer than you can shout), shots or fires.

Fig. 15 *Signalling 'yes' to a helicopter*

A two-way radio can be used anywhere and allows more than two people to have a discussion. VHF radios are better for outdoor use than UHF, because the radio waves travel twice the distance on open ground. UHF waves are better at penetrating solid objects, hence their use in avalanche transceivers.

Two-way radios operate on different frequencies, although they usually have pre-selected channels so that you need not tune them to a particular frequency. Each country allocates radio frequencies to different two-way services. VHF radios are either licensed or licence-free. In the US, the General Mobile Radio Service (GMRS) requires a license and the Family Radio Service (FRS) is free. In the UK, there are Licence-Free 446 radios and more powerful Professional Licenced Radios with similar channels. Rules vary from country to country – ensure that you have permission to use your VHF radio. Licence-free radios are fine for occasional use in close contact, e.g. for skiers, but their range is severely limited, they are fragile and they do not hold their charge well.

When choosing a channel for your team to operate on, privacy and range are your primary concerns. All radios in your group should be set to the same channel before you can communicate.

EMERGENCY FREQUENCIES

The internationally established emergency frequencies are vhf 156,800 Mhz channel 16. They are monitored by ships, aeroplanes and field stations.

THE TRANSMITTER
Never try to transmit on any radio-transmitting device if the antenna is not connected, as it may destroy the transmitter!

POWER

The greater the power the greater the range – a 1-watt radio is enough for 1.5km and a 2-watt radio up to 3.5km. Some radios have high and low power options – high power to transmit long distances. Use a taller antenna to further improve the range. Once the maximum range is exceeded, use a repeater, which is an intermediate receiver and transmitter located to relay messages to an out-of-sight location. They are not simple to use, because they receive and transmit on different frequencies. You must transmit on the frequency the repeater listens on and vice versa.

Fig. 16 *Arranging a pick-up from Antarctica using a two-way radio*

The author, Mount Fairweather, Alaska

Talking on the radio

- Keep conversations short and simple.
- Press the 'Push To Talk' (PTT) button to talk and release it to hear. The squelch control regulates speaker hiss when not transmitting, but too far and you will not hear anything.
- Hold the microphone close to your mouth, but do not shout.
- Use the phonetic alphabet.

TYPICAL RADIO CONVERSATION

'Base camp, base camp this is Alun, Alun, over.'	[Introduce yourself twice]
'Alun, Alun, this is base camp, base camp, go ahead.'	[Answer in the same way]
'Base camp, base camp, this is Alun ... we are running low on fuel, over.'	[If you require an answer say 'over'; if you do not say 'out'.]
'Alun, Alun this is base camp ... fuel will be sent up this evening with Tom, over.'	
'Base camp, base camp, this is Alun, Tom is bringing fuel this evening, thanks, out.'	[Wait for the answer before repeating back to the responder and completing with 'out']

SATELLITE PHONES

There is often a significant time delay on satellite phones, so be patient and use the same voice procedure as for the two-way radios.

SATELLITE PHONE SYSTEMS	
Name	**Use**
Inmarsat	Developed for intercontinental and marine communication. The position and height of geo-stationary satellites, and the fact that radio waves move in straight lines, results in 'dead ground' in Polar areas – communication is dependent upon the local topography above 70° latitude.
BGAN (Broadband Global Area Network)	A satellite, Internet and telephone service provided by Inmarsat. The service is currently accessible throughout Europe, Africa, the Middle East, Asia, North and South America.
Iridium	Uses orbiting satellites, providing global coverage.
Globalstar	The signal is only routed through more expensive satellites when a ground-based connection cannot be made.

SATELLITE PHONE USE

- Store the phone and battery separately in a warm place (LCD screens go blank at –20°C)
- Keep the phone, numbers and instructions in a waterproof container.
- Have the phone number and unlock code accessible.

OTHER COMMUNICATION SYSTEMS

Name	Use
Satellite pagers	Work through the Iridium satellite system. Log on to www.iridium.com to access instant messaging.
Mobile phones	Mobile phones work in most places (but rarely in remote mountains). Newer models incorporate GPS-type technology. Communication with a satellite phone requires a specific 'number' sequence, which differs between brands of phone.
Emergency Position Indicating Radio Beacon (EPIRB)	Alerts search and rescue services, sending a distress signal containing a unique code on 406 MHz, giving your details and approximate position. Also transmits on the 121.5 MHz homing frequency so that Search and Rescue aircraft can accurately locate you when they are near by. Use as a last resort in real emergencies only – misuse carries heavy penalties.
Personal Locator Beacon (PLB)	Essentially mini EPIRBs, registered to an individual.
Tracking and messaging systems – ARGOS	System of Low, Earth Orbiting (LEO) satellites. Regularly sends a ground position to a control centre when switched on. Operated on a cost recovery basis.

There are two types: disposable and rechargeable. Mixing them in equipment can result in leaks. Some types of larger batteries may require special packaging on aeroplanes.

DISPOSABLE BATTERIES

Zinc-carbon
These batteries are cheap and drain quickly.

Alkaline
Alkaline batteries are best for emergency devices, because they are inexpensive; have a temperature range to –20°C (alkaline-manganese batteries can be used to –30°C); the low discharge rate gives a long shelf life (6–8 years); and they are high capacity and dim slowly.

Lithium
These are the most powerful batteries you can buy, but they are expensive, with toxic contents. They are designed for high-drain devices like digital cameras. The shelf-life is 10+ years, and they excel in cold weather, but when done, they can quit without warning. They can cause some LED lamps to overheat and possibly damage the bulb – check the suitability to your device. Lithium batteries are not to be used for emergency devices.

RECHARGEABLE BATTERIES

Alkaline
Some rechargeable alkaline batteries can be recharged 10 times, but only with a specialist charger. They are great for high voltage, giving a brighter light in LED torches.

Nickel-cadmium (NiCad)
These batteries are cheap, but have been superceded by NIMH batteries.

Nickel metal hydride (NIMH)
NIMH batteries can be recharged up to 900 times! They are double the capacity; more environmentally friendly; do not suffer from memory effect and are cheaper than an equivalent NiCad. Discharge continues, even when not in use, so do not use for emergency devices.

Lithium ion (not to be confused with standard lithium batteries)
The low weight and high power of these batteries means that they are suitable for high-drain devices. The unique drawback is that they age from manufacture, regardless of whether they are charged.

RECHARGING BATTERIES
For best performance buy a 'smart' charger that can discharge the battery before charging it. Always mark rechargeable batteries and charge those that have similar amounts of discharge simultaneously. Try to buy batteries with the highest possible mAh rating.

Solar charging is generally slow, and the amount of electricity generated depends on the cell's size/surface, the Sun's strength, any cloud/mist/dust obstruction and the length of exposure. They can often be connected together to generate more electricity.

Solar panels have differing wattage – the higher the rating, the faster the device charges. To work out which charger is best, see the output rating of the charging adapter on the device that you wish to charge. If it doesn't show the wattage, it should show the ratings for amperes (amps) and volts (amperes x volts = watts).

Fig. 17 Solar chargers can charge devices directly or the separate battery (see www.selectsolar.co.uk).

MENUS

Food keeps you going, maintains warmth and adds to your enjoyment. On any long expedition, especially to altitude, it is a major challenge to provide meals that you can stomach; snacks that do not freeze keep your fuel levels up and taste nice for weeks at a time. Make food colourful, interesting and familiar (expect a recipe for six to serve four after a day's walking or climbing).

Do not create menus just around daily energy requirements, as you will end up with rations that are boring and inedible. Multivitamin and mineral supplements are required only when eating inadequate food for weeks.

ENERGY

You use more energy at altitude and in the cold, therefore increase your calorie intake to in excess of 4000 per day on expeditions. A diet high in carbohydrates (65 per cent) and lower in fat is best during periods of maximum exertion, because a high fat diet requires more oxygen to burn, which can hinder the process of acclimatisation.

COST

Balance the cost of transporting food against that of buying it in the destination country. Check what food is banned, e.g. it is illegal to take freeze-dried meat into Alaska and do not try to export beef to Nepal and India, or pork to Pakistan.

Take a large, insulated plastic mug, a plastic (not metal) spoon (a 'spork' is great) and a sharp knife. Tie a string between the cup and the spoon to avoid losing them. Also consider larger pots, a stove (see *Rucksack Guide: Mountain Walking and Trekking*), a pressure cooker and Thermos flasks to keep boiled water hot when not needed.

MAKING FOOD INTERESTING

- Sun-dried tomatoes, dried onions, mushrooms and peppers are lightweight and add flavour to a plain meal.
- Nuts are a great alternative to meat (peanuts and walnuts go rancid in the heat – try almonds and cashews).
- Toast and toss sesame, sunflower or pumpkin seeds into salads and main dishes.
- Add herbs and garlic to dried mashed potato.
- Use spreads (peanut, almond, cashew, soy nut or tahini).
- Heat up slivers of salami or dried beef to put into fajitas.
- Textured vegetable proteins (TVP) in soups and curries fool most people.
- Choose dark breads, like rye, which stay edible for about a week.
- Bring spices in small zip-lock bags or plastic bottles with screw tops: salt, pepper, garlic flakes and an 'all spice'. Mix them in a bag.
- Choose high-fibre, energy rich snacks such as oatcakes, dates, figs, low-fat grain bars, trail mix and prunes.
- Bring extra crackers and snacks.
- Make your own mixes, e.g. cereals, pancakes and scones.

FOOD AND COOKING

LOCAL FOOD		
Food type	Advice	Avoid
Fresh fruit and vegetables	Choose unblemished fruit. Wash it in sterilised water, wipe and peel.	Lettuce, unless you can soak it in potassium permanganate for 30 minutes and rinse.
Meat	Dried meats are great for long trips (salami keeps up to five days in summer).	Rare meat – cook until well done. Cover to keep any flies off.
Fish and shellfish	Can be hazardous at certain times of the year, even if well cooked.	Take local advice about seafood, but if in doubt, avoid it.
Dairy	Boil milk, unless you are sure it has been pasteurised or sterilised.	Cheeses and ice cream are often made from un-pasteurised milk – only buy from larger companies.

Fig. 18 Yak meat for sale in China. Ensure meat is freshly killed or take it with you live.

FOOD AVAILABILITY

Difficult to source	Food usually available in developing countries
• Instant 'Cup-a-Soups'	• Powdered fruit drinks
• Packets of spiced couscous	• Teabags
• Sachets of drinking chocolate	• Dried milk
• Luxury coffees	• Coffee
• Instant white sauce mix	• Ovaltine
• Cheese sauce mix	• Sliced cheese
• Bread sauce mix	• Tinned cheese
• Oatcakes	• Processed cheese
• Fruit cakes	• Cream cheese spread
• Tubes of vegetarian herb and mushroom paté	• Packet soups (limited flavours)
• Marmite	• Quick noodles and egg noodles
• Vegemite	• Basmati rice
• Packets of 'veggie burger' and 'soya mix'	• Pasta
• Instant custard	• Muesli
• Energy bars	• Porridge
• Sandwich and freezer bags	• Peanut butter
	• Tinned tuna
	• Chocolate bars
	• Boiled sweets
	• Dried fruit
	• Salted nuts

FOOD AND COOKING

Fig. 19 Pack everything carefully so that you know where it is. Make a detailed list and keep track of everything.

Specialist expedition foods are usually expensive and have a poor nutritional and calorific value (consider adding fresh produce to improve them).

SPECIALIST EXPEDITION FOODS		
Type	Advantage	Disadvantage
Dried	Cheaper than most specialist foods	Don't often taste or look anything like the description on the packet. Require a lot of cooking, except for pre-cooked and dehydrated cereals, rice and some vegetables.
Accelerated freeze-dried	Flavour and texture is preserved when rehydrated. Large selection of exotic meals are available. Look for re-hydrate in the bag brands where only boiled water is added.	The Dry Tech range are the best, but they are expensive (Fig. 20).
Pre-cooked meals in a bag	Taste better, do not have to be reconstituted, do not dirty the pan and can be eaten un-heated in an emergency.	Heavy to carry.

FOOD AND COOKING

Fig. 20 *The superb Dry Tech Range (Gareth Richardson)*

Any food with readily usable calories is energy food. Energy bars, gels and powders for drinks are convenient, light and compact, but they are expensive, have a strange texture and taste, and do not always provide the correct type of energy (a sudden hit of glucose triggers your insulin response, telling your body to store the energy). Nibble or sip high glucose bars to avoid a glucose crash.

PACKING AND STORAGE

- Plan the packing so you know who has what.
- Discard unnecessary packaging, keeping the instructions in a separate zip-lock plastic bag.
- Pack day ration packs containing breakfast and dinner, plus lunch and trail mix, and mark with the menu. Pack seven daily rations into a weekly pack and store in Ortlieb stuff bags. Assign each bag a particular week.
- Store extras, such as drinks, treats and spices, in separate bags; oils, cheese, butter and meat in another.
- Keep food away from fuel, toiletries, soap and other smelly items, and keep strong-smelling foods separate, for instance coffee and peppermint tea.
- Squeeze tubes and tinned food freeze solid in extreme weather.
- Olive oil, cheese, butter, some biscuits and chocolate tend to freeze solid, or melt and change state.
- Protect soft fruit and vegetables by packing in plastic containers (use these as mixing bowls later).
- Keep fruit and vegetables in a cool place at camp where air can circulate, e.g. hung in a net. Regularly sort them and discard those badly bruised, eating the less damaged fruit immediately. Green vegetables do not keep well – eat as soon as possible.
- Eggs last a week or longer if coated with grease or wrapped in cling-film.
- Keep meat as cool as possible, raising it to allow air circulation and protecting it from flies with muslin.

HYGIENE

- Cover all food and take care when buying uncovered food in villages.
- Wash your hands with water containing a disinfectant (antibacterial wipes are not enough). Check that local cooks do the same.
- Be meticulous about washing pans. Use your pasta/rice water for the first wash and rinse with clean water or wipe dishes clean with soft paper before they are washed in hot water. Detergent is unnecessary; a green scourer is sufficient.
- Dispose of kitchen and human waste well away from cooking areas and water sources. Burn and bury rubbish, which attracts scavengers, but remove cans and bottles for disposal elsewhere.

WATER

Tea and coffee, bottled beer and wine (wipe the tops) are usually safe. Keep your mouth closed in showers and clean your teeth with dry toothpaste. Do not drink water without boiling, iodine treatment or using a reliable filter, unless you are certain it is clean.

Purification

Prior to any purification, it is best to let the water stand for one hour to remove suspended particle matter, improving the effectiveness of the following sterilisation methods. Add $\frac{1}{4}$tsp/gal of aluminium sulphate (pickling powder), mix and wait for five minutes. Remove the clear water by pouring it through a coffee filter.

Boiling

Boiling is the most reliable if fuel and time is available. Boil water for several minutes to kill bugs; twice as long at higher altitudes, because of the lower boiling point. Boiling gives water a flat taste – aerate by pouring it from container to container for several minutes.

Iodine

Iodine is effective against viruses, bacteria and protozoans, except cryptosporidium cysts, and is available in tablet, liquid, crystal or resin form. The contact time should be one hour with cold water. Clean the bottle's neck after iodine is added. Iodine is easy to carry and fast to use, but leaves a taste. Eliminate by adding a small amount of powdered vitamin C to the water after treatment is complete (not before!). **Note:** Those with a history of thyroid disease or iodine allergy, the pregnant and the very young should avoid it.

Filters

Filters remove sand, clay and other matter, as well as organisms, protozoa, bacteria and parasites, but not viruses, unless using an iodine resin. However, as contact time is short, filters are not entirely reliable, and water must also be chemically treated or boiled. Filters do not require fuel, are fast for small quantities of water and give a better taste. Water left in the filter after use can freeze and crack it, rendering it inoperable or, worse, if it goes unnoticed allowing it to let harmful bugs through.

Chlorine

Chlorine destroys most bacteria, but it is less effective against viruses and cysts (e.g. Hepatitis A, Giardia and amoebic cysts). Organic matter deactivates chlorine and its effectiveness varies with acidity – iodine is safer.

Ultraviolet (UV-C) radiation pen

UV pens break down the DNA of viruses, bacteria and cysts, rendering them harmless. They are a fast and safe system for purifying clear water. However, discoloration, solids and debris limit the penetration of UV light. Ensure you use clear, unfrozen water or that it is purified beforehand.

Two doses of UV light kill 99.99 per cent of all harmful bugs. A set of four regular AA alkaline batteries last for about 20–40 uses, each for 1 pint of water at room temperature (the LED flashes red when the batteries are running low). The UV light tube wears after approximately 5000 uses, and must be returned to the manufacturer for replacement.

Water from snow and ice

To save fuel, dig a hole in a frozen lake or stream or use a 'solar water collector'. Spread a dark plastic bag over a 0.3m hole, packing clean snow over the raised margins. Punch a small hole in the centre and place a large pan underneath. The Sun heats the dark plastic and water collects in the pan (20 pints of clean snow makes 2 pints of water). It is more efficient to melt ice than snow.

Fig. 21

See also *Rucksack Guides to Winter Mountaineering* and *Alpinism*. Non-climbing equipment routinely fails, so know everything about it; be able to take it apart and re-build it. Take your own mug, sleeping mat, possibly a spare stove, food and extra hats and gloves for porters. Some equipment is best bought or hired in the host country, e.g. large cook tents, base camp stoves, cooking utensils and fuel.

In remote mountains the temperatures often remain low – add a shadowy mountain face and you require extra layers. The wind is more problematic than the temperature. If you are going to the Polar Regions – even in the summertime – prepare for temperatures as low as –30°C combined with strong winds.

- Wear just enough to stay dry and comfortable. Avoid starting out warm, then sweating. Immediately add layers when taking a break or standing still.
- Rain is unlikely to be an issue at altitude or in the Polar Regions, so consider a windproof, rather than a waterproof.
- Choose black items to aid heat absorption.
- Avoid open-face fabrics (e.g. fleece) as outerwear, as frost builds up.
- Pay particular attention to extremities; exposed skin can freeze in minutes.
- Climbers attempting peaks such as Vinson in Antarctica require a one-piece down suit or a down jacket and down salopettes, in addition to all the accoutrements necessary for ultra cold weather climbing.
- A neoprene mask that covers the mouth and nose, and wraps around the neck is essential wear in all Polar Regions and on peaks over 7000m.

EQUIPMENT AND TECHNIQUES

Fig. 22 *The wind is often more of a problem than the cold (Cotopaxi, Ecuador).*

EXPERT TIP

Shaun Hutson
shaun@sphutson.com

'Just because you have had very cold feet and hands in oxygen-rich lower altitudes without frostbite, don't think you can apply the same approach to higher altitudes. Frostbite is often the result of ignoring a bit of the body.'

- Avoid sunburn by wearing a neckerchief over the mouth and nose on hot glaciers.
- Plastic boots have a liner that can be removed and dried, so they are better for multi-day trips.
- A soft and large boot that allows you to flex the toes helps to avoid frostbite.

Sleeping bags for the cold

Take a close-fitting, mummy-style bag with a hood, a baffle over the zip and a draft collar at the neck. There are three options, each with advantages and dis-advantages in terms of price, weight, and volume:

1 **An expedition bag**, e.g. Mountain Equipment range.
2 **A three-season bag** augmented with a vapour barrier liner, or a Gore-tex bivvy bag that gives an extra operating range of 5–10°C.
3 **Two smaller bags** combine a two-season down bag with a two- or three-season synthetic bag. Ensure the extra bag fits over the down bag without compressing it (although weight and bulk are increased).

On prolonged trips in extreme cold, perspiration condenses and ice crystals slowly build up inside the bag's insulation, wetting the bag and reducing its loft.

- Wear fewer clothes to generate body heat inside your sleeping bag, driving the moisture out.
- Whenever you can, drape your bag in the Sun to dry it out (even when it is below freezing, as moisture is removed by sublimation of the ice).

Fig. 23 Coping with the cold in Greenland

A vapour barrier liner (VBL) is an impermeable layer designed to trap moisture close to the skin, shutting down the body's sweating response. They prevent evaporative heat loss, slow dehydration and keep moisture out of your insulation layer. Do not use them directly against the skin, as evaporation at the skin surface cools you down.

For sleeping bags
Sleeping in a VBL is miserable, as you end up being damp, but as your bag remains dry, you are at least warm and damp, rather than dry and cold. One disadvantage is that you are unable to dry clothes next to your body.

For your feet
The closed cell foam liner and plastic shell in plastic boots prevent water from escaping; therefore, above 7000m and in polar climates VBLs are useful. However, many purpose-built socks are slippery and tempt you to tie your boots tighter, restricting blood flow. You must wear a lightweight sock inside them, yet wet socks next to your skin will increase your chances of blisters, trench foot and infection. Use foot powder and rub in antiperspirant gel each morning. RBH Designs have a thick and thin fleece with a VBL inbetween, which seems to overcome these problems (www.rbhdesigns.com).

EQUIPMENT AND TECHNIQUES

Most mountain areas, with exceptions like Borneo, have well-defined trails through villages and across mountain passes. Popular trekking trails, especially in Nepal, have accommodation in tea houses, although the standards of food and hygiene vary considerably. Cooking meals is slow in teahouses, so get up early, have a hot drink and walk for several hours before stopping for breakfast.

BASE CAMP

The benefits of a pleasant base camp should not be underestimated. A base camp should be a place to relax, recuperate and celebrate special occasions, but it should not be so comfortable that you don't want to leave. Use a mess tent or a large sheet of polythene as a communal area. Keep fuel away from the tents and consider carrying a fire blanket or a sand bucket. Ensure stoves are well ventilated – smoke aggravates everyone's eyes, noses and throats, which will already be suffering because of the dry mountain air.

Fig. 24 A pleasant base camp can make or break an expedition (Ladakh).

TOILETS

Waste does not degrade easily at altitude or low temperatures.

- Erect a toilet tent with a deep trench 50m away from the cook tent and all water sources. A hole 2–3m deep lasts several months.

- Carry a bucket and a toilet seat if you want luxury and you are at base camp for extended periods.

- Cover each deposit with earth or ash; 'flame' it periodically using kerosene.

- Do not use disinfectant as it kills the bacteria necessary for decomposition.

- Dispose of toilet paper and sanitary towels in a bin (carry it out later).

- Remember that bears and other scavengers are attracted by smells.

- In popular trekking areas it might be regulation to carry all rubbish and toilet waste away with you in a leak-proof receptacle (e.g. in any North American National Park, the Antarctic and the Sagarmatha National Park, Nepal).

Fig. 25 Asian cooks and porters will often not use a western toilet.

TENTS		
Type of tent	Advantages	Disadvantages
Three-season	Good for short stays	Do not stand up to high winds or the weight of snow build-up. Too ventilated to provide shelter.
Four-season geodesic dome	Strong poles, snow valances and a roofline that sheds snow Shed snow well and provide efficient interior space	Heavier, increased condensation
Single skin pyramid tent	Lightweight	Colder, require staking out and floors require sealing e.g. with a space blanket

PEGS

- Regular tent pegs are useless unless buried horizontally.
- For overnight camping, use ice axes, skis and trekking poles to guy the tent.
- For longer stays, use snow stakes and sections of bamboo, or bury stuff sacs full of snow.
- Use Abolokov threads or ice screws on bare ice.
- Bring extra poles and pole splints for any pole breaks that may occur.

CONDENSATION

- Brush ice particles from expired breath off the tent in the morning.
- Hang a frost liner inside the tent, which allows moisture to pass through.
- Venting the tent decreases ice build up, but makes for a colder night.
- Use a small brush to clear snow off your clothes, gear and boots before getting into the tent; a sponge cleans up spills and melted condensation.

THE PERFECT SITE ON SNOW

- Is sheltered from the wind and avalanches.
- Faces south, giving longer days and more sunlight.
- Should be near a lake or stream.
- Probe the entire area for crevasses while roped up.
- Establish paths around the tents and to the toilet.
- Dig or stamp out a tent platform (with snowshoes or skis), otherwise the melting and refreezing of snow forms a trough, which is uncomfortable.
- In warm conditions, a tent left in one place for days ends up on a pedestal and may have to be moved.

If you cannot find a sheltered site:

- Dig a hole 1m deep to reduce wind impact.
- Build a thick teardrop shaped wall (Fig. 14) the same height as the tent and as far away from it as it is high.
- Or build snow mounds up the tent sides (with someone pushing from inside the tent to prevent it collapsing). As the snow thaws and refreezes, you get an insulated hybrid tent-snow shelter.
- Shovel wind-blown snow away to prevent the tent poles breaking or asphyxiation.
- Dig a deep, rectangular pit in the tent porch for removing boots (Fig. 26).

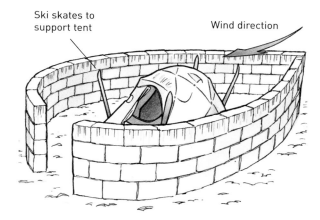

Ski skates to support tent

Wind direction

Fig. 26 *Build a wall to protect your tent from the winter winds.*

A COMMUNAL TENT ON SNOW

- Dig a pit for your kitchen at least 2m in diameter x 1m deep (for four to six people).
- Pile the excavated snow around the perimeter and pack it down.
- You can carve out seats and benches and then erect your tent over the hole (Fig. 27).

Wind direction

Fig. 27

Fig. 28 A communal cook tent (Mountain Hardwear Kiva tent, Greenland)

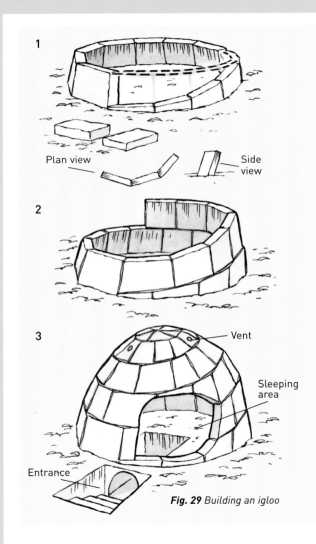

1

Plan view

Side view

2

3

Vent

Sleeping area

Entrance

Fig. 29 Building an igloo

BUILDING AN IGLOO

It takes around two hours to build an igloo (Fig. 29):

1 Draw a circle 2m across and pack the snow.

2 Set up a quarry area close to the circle, dig for the best snow and don't underestimate the number of blocks required. Cut blocks 75cm x 30cm (bigger blocks do not necessarily make for a stronger igloo due to the extra weight).

3 Create a circular ramp with a snow saw. Start the second row by placing the first block on the ramp's lowest point.

4 Lean each block towards the igloo centre (supported both by the blocks beneath and to the side – Fig 29.2). The top of each block should point to the centre.

5 Lay the remainder close to horizontal overhead.

6 Excavate, digging a tunnel under the wall to create an entrance (Fig. 29.3).

7 Fill any cracks with snow to create a very strong structure and dig inside to increase the floor area.

Marker wands can help you to find the route in poor visibility (Mramornaya Stena, Pamirs)

MARKER WANDS

Essential for marking routes in poor visibility, after a storm or in a crevassed area or for marking the routes to tents, toilets and food stores. Take 20–200, depending on your trip. Mark danger areas with two wands in an X shape.

TOILETS ON SNOW

- Make a personal hole as needed. Dig a wall for privacy around a group toilet area, using a marker wand to indicate when it is occupied.
- Kick snow over urine stains (urination on snow is forbidden in Antarctica, as the stains remain on the ice, given it never melts and there is virtually no precipitation to cover it).
- Burn toilet paper in a tin can or pack it out.

KEEPING WARM AND DRY

Change into dry clothes as soon as camp is set up. Insulated booties with closed-cell foam insoles keep your feet warmer than boots. Don't use your sleeping mat outside as it gets wet. Carry a small closed-cell foam pad to sit on.

Limit alcohol intake, as it thins your blood and inhibits the body's ability to warm itself. With 10+ hours in the tent you will need to urinate, but do not wait to urinate until morning – energy is wasted keeping the extra fluid warm. Keep a pee bottle (store in your bag for warmth and to prevent it freezing).

DRYING CLOTHES AND BOOTS

Place gloves, socks and the next day's clothes inside your sleeping bag, but not large articles of clothing (they wet the bag, making it cold).

Open boots as wide as possible when you remove them, making it easier to put them on in the morning. Put them in a breathable stuff sack placing a bottle of warm water inside. Sleep with the insoles on your chest.

Put inners from plastic boots in a breathable bag or add a hot water bottle.

Sleeping

- Snack before bed so that your body generates heat during the night. Get warm by exercising for several minutes before bedtime.

- Avoid wearing layers, as they hold body heat close rather than warming up the inside of the sleeping bag, leaving hands and feet cold.

- Raise cold feet to allow warm air to flow to them. Put a bottle of warm water in the foot of your sleeping bag an hour before you get in.

- Use two sleeping pads on snow, as insulation from the ground is more important than insulation from the cold air.

- Keep at least one water bottle in or under the sleeping bag.

- Sleep with your face outside the bag to reduce moisture build-up.

- Frequently changing position allows blood to circulate to compressed tissues.

- If you wake up cold, eat some food; have a Thermos of hot drink in your tent and exercise.

In the morning

The few degrees of warmth trapped by a sealed up tent increase condensation – vent your tent as much as possible at night. Stay in the sleeping bag for as long as you can while cooking breakfast, packing, etc. If you have left your boots outside your sleeping bag, remove the insoles and warm them in your sleeping bag or next to your body.

EXPERT TIP

John Russel
www.greenlandexpedition. com

'Pitched well, lightweight single-skin pyramid tents with a single centre pole (even a trekking pole), are surprisingly robust and provide a lot of space. On snow, dig a pit with seats to create a spacious communal tent and cooking area. It is good for morale, and will also cut down on condensation in your sleeping tent.'

Sea ice forms from seawater when the temperature drops below −1.8°C (35.24°F) for a long time. There isn't room for salt molecules to collect in its close-knit structure and they are rejected back into the sea as the ice forms.

- 'Land-fast' ice, or 'fast ice', is flat sea ice that has frozen along coasts extending out from the land to the sea.
- 'Drift' ice floats on the water's surface. When packed together in large masses, it is called 'pack' ice, which may float freely or be blocked by 'fast' ice while drifting past.
- Icebergs form out of chunks of fresh water from ice shelves or glaciers that have 'calved' into the sea.
- The actual coastline may be tens of kilometres inland from the ice shelf (glacier's snout), which can drop down quite steeply to meet the sea ice.
- Be careful close to the shelf edge in poor visibility.
- The sea's tidal movement creates cracks between the sea ice and the ice shelf – always consider them as fresh.

INTERPRETING SEA ICE
- Treat all ice with suspicion, particularly when buried under fresh snow. However, surface ice is often supported by the water and can take more weight than you would imagine.
- Opaque, 'white' ice that resists several hard hits is weight bearing.
- Black ice is highly dangerous, as is sea ice thinner than 75cm (30in).
- When walking, beware that cracks and seals' breathing holes may be covered with snow.
- Check ice conditions with locals before travelling on to it.

A frozen sea, Greenland

AIRDROPS

In some Polar Regions, e.g. Greenland National Park, advance airdropping of supplies is not permitted.

- Pick the drop zone carefully for suitability to the aircraft.
- Trample or mark a cross on the ground at the drop zone a minimum of 100m from campsites.
- Pack all supplies to survive the impact. Use brightly painted 50l plastic drums for easy location.
- Fill each barrel with items of similar density and hardness. Individually bubble wrap every tin and packet and triple bag every portion of food.

SLED (PULK) HAULING

- Inexpensive plastic sleds flex and can crack.
- Purpose-built fibreglass and plastic pulks around 1m–2.6m are available, dependent upon the trip length, the number of crevasses and the snow consistency.
- In soft snow, the pulk should be 2m or longer to prevent it from sinking and to make crossing crevasses safer.
- The bottom should be ridged (on plastic models) or have runners (on more expensive composites) to maintain a straight line and prevent sideways sliding while traversing slopes. However, they have limited effect on hard snow or ice. In this situation, the best strategy is to pick a course perpendicular to the slope and use crampons.
- Protect the bottom of your pulk at all costs.

Fig. 30 *A sled hauling system*

Packing the sled

- Keep heavyweight items at the bottom of the sled to stop it tipping over.
- Purpose-built covers can have a zip along the length of the sledge.
- In wet areas, be sure to empty any standing water in the bottom of the sledge every day.
- Secure the load with a zigzag of rope or bungee cord (you require the right length to create the correct tension).

MOUNTAINEERING IN POLAR REGIONS

The amount of daylight varies far more in polar regions. Even at 60° latitude there is almost 24 hour daylight in midsummer. Many expeditions prefer 'night' travel when snow surfaces are more likely to be frozen, but you should still schedule sensible work and rest periods.

Towing a sled (Fig. 30)

- Ropes are light and good on flat surfaces, whereas poles (traces) give you more control when travelling downhill and guiding the sledge through difficult sections. Poles can be made of bamboo, aluminium or fibreglass.

- A sledge harness distributes the strain between the waist, chest and shoulders; a waist belt will not do, but a comfortable, well-padded, large volume rucksack with a chest strap is almost as good. Clip directly into the strap that ascends over your shoulder, just above the waist belt, or sew in purpose-made loops.

- Alternatively, thread the rope around the rucksack, just above the waist belt.

- Create an 'X' in the ropes by tying them together one-third of the way from the sledge to maintain a stable pull.

- Do not attach the haul line to ice axe loops on the back of the rucksack – it hunches the hauler over.

- Bungee cord can stop the sled jerking.

TOWING TIPS

- Your legs are strongest, so use them.
- Leaning forward enables you to overcome many small obstructions.
- Placing weight in your rucksack increases your effective hauling mass on difficult terrain.

TOWING TECHNIQUES

Problem	Solution
In dangerous crevassed areas	Keep close to your partner, but not so close that you would fall into the same crevasse. Attach the sledge to a trailing rope via a prusik to prevent it following the skier into the crevasse.
To keep the sled tracking on hard snow	Attach steel fins to the base with pop riveting or butterfly bolts (they can be reversed when not in use).
On steep slopes with deep snow	Make a rising traverse, which is less strenuous. Descend a straight line with the sledge in front if possible.
When side-slipping	Someone should ski alongside to prevent the sled running too far forward or down the slope. Attach a rope from the rear of the sledge to the person behind.

KITES AND SAILS

These range from ex-military parachutes to purpose-made, highly sophisticated adjustable kites. Designed for hauling loads, they work best when the wind direction is blowing towards where you wish to go. Under the right conditions they give very fast travelling times.

Note: The risk of injury is higher than with standard hauling.

Fixed lines allow mountaineers to quickly cross or ascend dangerous or steep terrain. Pre-stretched rope is better than dynamic rope for avoiding stretch, and kernmantle is better than hawser-laid. The ascender's grip is affected by the rope diameter, the way it is made (hawser laid or kernmantle), the material (nylon or polypropelene), and how icy it is.

- Mark the anchor points with wands to locate them after heavy snowfall and protect the rope from abrasion on edges.
- Place intermediate anchors for more climbers to use the line and lessen the weight of rope on one anchor (there should only be one climber between each fixed section).
- Always position anchors at a change in direction and at the top of any difficulties.
- Bury anchors and check them frequently.
- Leave some slack between points to reduce vector forces, allow movement of the climber and minimise side-loading of the anchor.
- For fixed ropes on the flat (crevassed ground) use two cows' tails.
- Lines should be frequently inspected for damage.

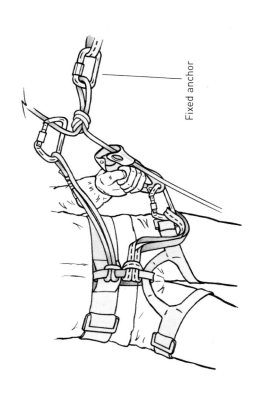

Fixed anchor

Fig. 31 *Ascending fixed lines. Lark's foot an ascender and a sling and krab on to your harness. To descend, use a figure of eight descender or reverse going up.*

REMOTE EXPEDITION PECULIARITIES

It is best to find a bridge or camp until the river subsides. The next best thing is to carry an inflatable raft or inner tube. Rivers fed by glacial melt water drop during the night but may be impassable by midday. Even a shin-deep fast-flowing river can build up in front of you as you are crossing – wait for morning, after the cool night has reduced the river flow, or for a suitable time after a storm.

- Use the map to gauge where best to cross. The widest part is usually the shallowest – upstream there may be less water flowing into the main river.
- Cross below any dangers, such as waterfalls, and beware of bends – the outside bank can be undercut and the water deeper and much faster flowing.
- Unbuckle rucksacks or remove and bring them across on a rope.
- Keep boots on so that you don't lose your footing.
- If you are crossing alone, use a pole or stick.
- It is safer to cross as a team. Use the strongest person to break the flow away from the weaker members. Keep the strongest and biggest people at the wedge apex to create an eddy to the rear.
- Alternatively, use the methods shown in Fig. 32.

USING A ROPE

The security offered by a rope is often illusory. Never fasten someone on to a rope, as they may be dragged under. If the planning for the trip reveals the potential for river crossing, practice beforehand and ensure you are equipped with a throw-line.

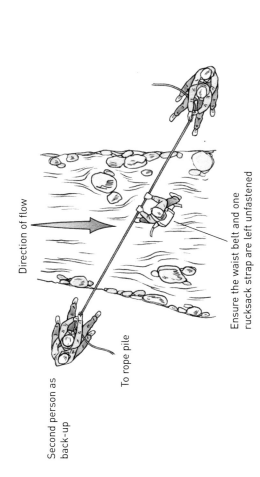

Direction of flow

Ensure the waist belt and one rucksack strap are left unfastened

Second person as back-up

To rope pile

Fig. 32 A tensioned hand line angled across the river. Find a bridge rather than take the risk of crossing a river.

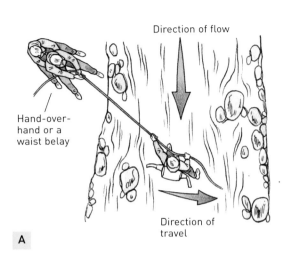

Direction of flow

Hand-over-hand or a waist belay

Direction of travel

A

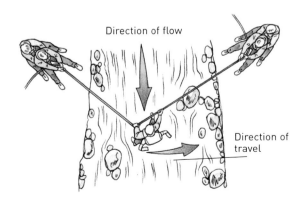

Direction of flow

Direction of travel

B

C

Direction of flow

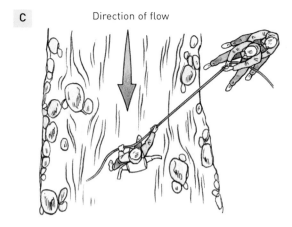

Fig. 33 *Ropes and water do not mix*

FROZEN RIVERS

Frozen rivers are best avoided, but if you must cross it is safer in the morning. As a rough guide, 2.5cm of black or white ice probably holds if you lie down and crawl, 5cm probably holds you walking, while 15cm is safe.

- Spread the group out or cross one at a time without a rucksack.

- The lead person probes with a ski pole. Poke the ice fairly hard. If the probe goes through, turn back and find another route.

- Solid ice produces a different sound (tick) versus thin ice over an air pocket (tock). Release all rucksack straps to allow a rapid jettison and keep a knife handy.

Fig. 34 Crossing a swollen river in Nepal

SHOULD YOU GO THROUGH THE ICE

- Extend your arms forward over the ice, kick your legs up to get level in the water and work forward on to the ice by kicking and carefully pulling with the arms.

- Use a knife to pull on. If the ice breaks, keep doing the above process until firm ice is reached.

- After pulling the entire body on to firm ice, carefully roll or edge toward shore, distributing body weight as widely as possible.

RESCUING A VICTIM FROM ICE

Throw a rope to the person who fell through. Do not approach the hole. Lie down and extend objects towards the hole using skis poles or anything you can grab hold of. Erect a tent and warm and dry the person.

Fig. 35 Crossing a river in Ladakh

THE ENVIRONMENT

Most of the world's mountains are in special places. Rubbish is not particularly environmentally damaging in high mountains and the only other people who see it are other mountaineers but how many of us like climbing through a rubbish tip? Mountains require special treatment in order to preserve the qualities that make them attractive to us. Learn to tread lightly, take responsibility for your actions and think of the overall good of the area and those who follow you.

DO:

- Travel in smaller teams to lessen your impact, on the environment and the locals.
- Educate your cooks and porters – explain that without a clean environment tourism will decline.
- Remove your own and other people's waste.
- Burn only burnable or non-toxic waste (not plastic). Only burn in base camp after having spoken with your Sirdar, and ask him to arrange the fire.
- Ensure there is fuel left at the end of the trip for the final fire and that everything is thoroughly destroyed.
- Carry out all non-burnable and toxic waste. Ensure that removed waste reaches its destination (porters may dump it).
- Purify stream water rather than buying bottled water.
- Dispose of human waste at least 200m from water sources or carry it away. Use lime in a deep pit to sterilise the waste.
- Use established campsites whenever possible.
- Reduce the impact on forested areas by using only deadwood for fires.
- Use cotton sacks rather than plastic bags.

DON'T:

- Build cairns or walls – if you do, take them down afterwards.
- Leave old batteries – take them home.
- Cut corners on tracks and take care not to collapse riverbanks.
- Wash dishes directly in streams.
- Feed animals – it alters their natural foraging habits.
- Build fires.

Fig. 36 *Polluting water and stressing wildlife are two of the greatest impacts in remote areas.*

Sadly, the wild places of the world are increasingly being turned into theme parks, as tourism tries to make them accessible to all, but there are still places for the intrepid traveller who wishes to experience the world, and not just see it.

EUROPE
Masses of mountains, but only several can be considered 'remote'.

Caucasus (Armenia, Azerbaijan, Georgia, various parts of Russia and several other 'territories') Stretching from the Black Sea to the Caspian Sea, and comparable in character to the European Alps, peaks average 1830–2743m (6004–8999ft), with Mount Elbrus at 4413m (14,478ft). The weather is seldom settled, particularly in the west, where the climate is affected by the Black Sea.

Iceland Several volcanic peaks and ice fields, which make a great first ski crossing. Expect very cold, wet and windy conditions year-round.

AFRICA
Atlas Mountains (Algeria, Morocco, Tunisia) The most northerly of Africa's mountains. The highest peaks (twelve over 3960m/12,992ft) are in the western range, the High Atlas. The highest is Mount Toubkal (4165m/ 13,665ft). There is good trekking in the Rif Mountains.

Rwenzori (Democratic Republic of Congo, Uganda) Six high glaciated massifs, including Africa's third-highest peak, Mount Margherita, at 5109m (15,762ft).

The Virunga Mountains (DR Congo, Rwanda, Uganda) Eight volcanoes, the highest being Mount Karisimbi (4507m/14,787ft).

The Aberdare Range (Kenya) Heavily forested uplands with an average elevation of 3810m (2367ft). Oldoinyo la Satima 4001m (13,120ft) is the highest. Mount Kenya (5199m/17,057ft), the second-highest mountain in Africa, lies several kilometres to the east.

Simien Mountains (Ethiopia) A vast, hilly plateau rising occasionally to form higher groups, separated by broad river valleys. Several peaks rise above 4000m (13,123ft), including Ras Dashen at 4533m (14,872ft).

Cameroon Mountains (Cameroon, Central African Republic, Chad, Nigeria) An isolated volcanic mass, towering higher than any other mountains in Western Africa. On the island of Malabo, Pico de Santa Isabel rises to 3008m (9869ft).

The Tibesti Mountains (Chad) The largest and highest range in the Sahara desert, formed by a group of dormant volcanoes. Emi Koussi is highest at 3445m (11,302ft).

Madagascar Large island off the southeast coast of Africa. Its granite peaks form big walls, the highest being Maromokotro (2876m/9436ft).

Mount Baker, Rwenzori Mountains, Uganda

ASIA

Himalaya (Afghanistan, Bhutan, China, India, Nepal, Pakistan) Contains nine of the world's highest peaks. Sikkim, Kumaon, Garhwal, Kulu, Lahul-Spiti, Padar, Zanskar and Ladakh all have many 5000–7000m (16,404–22,966ft) peaks. Look also at the Kangchenjunga, Mahalungur, Langtang, Rolwaling, Ganesh, Manaslu, Annapurna, Dhaulagiri, Nilgiri and Kanjiroba ranges of Nepal. West Nepal is also opening up, but the approaches are quite long. Three 8000m (26,247ft) peaks, but there are many lower peaks and other areas where it is possible to make first ascents, new routes and remote treks.

Pamirs, Congling Mountains (Afghanistan, Kyrgyzstan, Pakistan, Tajikistan) Wild and remote, with many peaks above 6000m (19,865ft). The highest point is Communism Peak (7495m/24,590ft).

Tien Shan (Kazakhstan, Kyrgyzstan, Pakistan, western China) Boundless, unexplored peaks, with more than thirty circa 6000m (19,685ft). They are dominated by Pobeda Peak (7439m/24,406ft) and Khan-Tengri (7010m/22,999ft).

Karakoram (China, India, Pakistan) The Baltoro Glacier and Hushe Valleys have many rock towers. The Batura Glacier, the Biafo Hispar Glacier and the remote Shimshal region have many interesting possibilities and the Hindu Raj, west of Gilgit, has many sub-6000m peaks.

Hindu Kush (Afghanistan, Pakistan) Around 24 summits above 7000m (22,966ft); the highest is Tirich Mir (7690m/25,230ft).

Hindu Raj (northern Pakistan) A little-known range. Its highest peak is Koyo Zom, 6872m (22,546ft).

Xinjiang (People's Republic of China) Has 7000m (22,966ft) peaks in the Kongur Range, including Muztagh Ata (7546m/24,757ft). The Bogda Ola Range has smaller 4000–5400m (13,123–17,717ft) peaks, and the recently opened, but remote, Kunlun Mountains offer many new peaks.

Sichuan (western China) Noted for Minya Gonga (7500m/24,606ft) and a number of lower peaks. There is climbing and trekking in the Gonga Shan, Chola Shan and Siguniang Shan (all around 6000m/19,685ft).

Qinghai (People's Republic of China) Non-technical 6000–6500m (19,685–21,325ft) peaks with a long trek in.

Yunnan (People's Republic of China) Has several 6000–6500m peaks. Approach is difficult.

Mongolia Lower in elevation than other Asian mountain groups, it is very remote, and much time and planning are required for its approach. In the isolated western province of Uvs two dominating twin peaks, Mount Kharkhiraa (4037m/13,245ft) and Mount Turgen (3678m/12,067ft), and their accompanying mountain passes, offer wonderful trekking opportunities. The highest peak is Gora Belukha (4506m/14,783ft).

Siberia (Russia) Ranges are small compared to Central and Southern Asian counterparts, yet are remote and rugged, with some spectacular isolated peaks. Major ranges include the Cherskiy Range, Kamchatka Peninsula, Kinghan Range, Sayan Mountains, Sikhote-Alin, Stanovoi Range, Ural Mountains and Yablonovyy Range.

Bhutan Almost entirely mountainous. Climbing and trekking is very expensive – this is not a place for expeditions on a shoestring.

Mustang (Nepal) Elevation of more than 2500m (8202ft). Has been completely untouched by modern life for centuries.

Siguniang Mountain, Sichuan Province of the People's Republic of China

SOUTH AMERICA

Andes (Argentina, Bolivia, Chile, Colombia, Ecuador, Peru, Venezuela) One of the world's great mountain ranges, rising to well over 6500m (21,325ft). The Andes fall somewhere between the mountains of Europe and the wild peaks of Asia in height, difficulty and access, making them ideal for experienced mountaineers aspiring to more remote peaks without the bureaucratic problems of a Himalayan expedition.

Bolivia The ideal country for a first visit, with a very stable climate and both hard and easy peaks. The Cordillera Quimsa Cruz, south of Bolivia's capital La Paz, comprises more than eighty peaks above 5000m (16,404ft). From the range's northern edge, multi-day treks lead to remote and striking rock spires and snow-capped peaks.

Beyond the Andes Mountaineering possibilities are limited to the coastal ranges of Brazil, isolated mountains in Venezuela, e.g. Roraima, and the sub- Andean ranges, e.g. the Sierra de Còrdoba.

Patagonia (Argentina and southern Chile) Some of the most difficult big walls in the world, such as Fitzroy and the Torres del Paine. Much of it is unknown and unexplored. The entire range is blanketed by two long, narrow ice caps. The weather becomes worse as you travel south, changing from Mediterranean in the north to 'Scottish' in the far south.

Alpamayo, Peruvian Andes

NORTH AMERICA

Alaska Range (United States) Some of the longest mountain routes in the world. The highest peak is Mount Denali at 6,193m (20,320ft). Harsh weather and heavy snowfall has created large glaciers.

The Brooks Range (Canada, US) Remote range stretching across Northern Alaska, from the Chukchi Sea, to the Yukon border. The mountains are not especially high, the highest peak being Mount Isto at 2762m (9062ft). The higher slopes are snow- and ice-clad for much of the year.

Wrangell Mountains (US) In southeast Alaska, they rise above an immense snowy wilderness, and average around 3660m (12,008ft). Best-known for several higher peaks, including Mounts Blackburn at 4995m (16,388ft), Sanford at 4950m (16,240ft) and Wrangell at 4560m (14,961ft). They are mostly non-technical, but serious, requiring long expeditionary approaches in often challenging weather.

Saint Elias Mountains (Canada, US) The highest coastal range in the world, with hundreds of sharp, ice-clad peaks rising above sea-level glaciers. Includes the highest mountain in Canada, Mount Logan (5960m/19,554ft).

The Fairweather Range (US) The southern continuation of the Saint Elias Mountains. Towers near the sea and forms extensive glaciers. The highest is Mount Fairweather (4663m/15,299ft).

Baffin Island (Canada) An Arctic wilderness located in the extreme northeast. Access is by boat, dog sled, float-plane or ski-plane. The highest peak is Tête Blanche (2156m/7073ft), but the most famous is Mount Asgard (2011m/6598ft).

British Columbia Coast Range (Canada) An immense snowy massif, filled with glaciers that stretch for miles with many steep faces rising up to c.1500m (4921ft). Mount Waddington is the highest at 4019m (13,186ft).

OTHER

New Zealand
The Southern Alps Run along the western side of the South Island, with many smaller peaks with complicated access. Aoraki/Mount Cook is the highest point 3754m (12,316ft).

Australasia/Oceania
The Malay Archipelago A number of interesting destinations such as Borneo, Java, Sulawesi and Sumatra.

New Guinea
The Owen Stanley Range (Papua New Guinea) Part of the central mountain chain. The highest peak is Mount Victoria at 4072m (13,360ft).

Pegunungan Maoke (Irian Jaya, Indonesia) Formerly known as the Central Range, many peaks lie above 3660m (12,000ft).

The Bismarck Range (Papua New Guinea) The highest point is Mount Wilhelm at 4509m (14,793ft).

Sudirman Range (Province of Papua, Indonesia) The western part of the Maoke Mountains. Includes Oceania's highest peak, Puncak Jaya (Mount Carstensz) at 4884m (16,024ft).

Antarctica
The Queen Maud Mountains A major mountain range lying between the Beardmore and Reedy Glaciers. The highest peak is Mount Ellsworth at 2925m (9596ft).

The Sentinel Range Forming the northern part of the Ellsworth Mountains and lying north of the Minnesota Glacier. Many peaks rise over 4000m (13,123ft), with the highest, Vinson, at 4897m (16,066ft).

Greenland
The highest mountains are in the Watkins Range. Large pack ice limits the sea approach, so expeditions typically require airlifts. Smaller peaks can be climbed all year round if accessed by dog sled or ski.

The three primary peaks are all nunataks (nunataqs), high mountains protruding through glacial ice. The highest is Gunnbjorn's Fjeld (3700m/ 12,139ft). The Schweizer Land Mountains are located south of the Watkins Range; the highest is Mont Forel (3360m/ 11,024ft).

A more accessible alternative are the smaller mountains in the far south, with a longer climbing season and easy access from Narssarsuaq. The highest is Mount Patuersoq (2740m/ 8989ft). The west coast mountains are also reasonably accessible, as much of the coast is approachable year-round by sea. Godthaab, Greenland's capital, has a large subsidiary ice cap from which rises the west coast's highest peak, Mount Atter (2189m/7185ft).

The Arctic
Only 1125km (699 miles) from the North Pole, a cluster of Arctic islands make up the Norwegian archipelago of Svalbard. The west coast is ice-free during the summer months. The largest and most mountainous island is Spitsbergen, which has sharp peaks averaging 1000m (3281ft), though some exceed 1500m (4921ft).

And the rest ...
Don't forget the following mountain ranges: Altay Mountains (Turkey); Sulaiman Mountains (Pakistan); Safed Koh (Afghanistan-Pakistan border); Zagros Mountains (Iran, Iraq); and several ranges in Yugoslavia and Poland.

Greenland: the future of remote mountaineering without altitude problems.

Expedition planning is not rocket science, but it is easy to underestimate the time and effort involved – forget a stove or get the wrong visa and your trip could be over. There are many sources of information on past expeditions:

- **The Alpine Club (AC) library** Numerous reports, journals and an extensive collection of mountaineering books. It has a computerised index of Himalayan peaks above 6000m (19,685ft) from which, for a small charge, all known references to a peak can be obtained.

- **Journals** The most useful are *The Alpine Club Journal*, *The American Alpine Journal* and the *Himalayan Journal* (all available at the AC Library).

- **Magazines** The 'Mountain Info' section in *Climb* magazine is very useful.

- **The Expedition Advisory Centre** Based at the Royal Geographical Society, London, the centre produces tailor-made information packs for mountain areas, keeps a library of expedition reports and runs lectures and seminars.

- **The British Mountaineering Council** A range of information sheets on permits etc. and reports from BMC-supported expeditions.

- **Other climbers** However famous they are, I can guarantee they will help – they are, first and foremost, trekkers and mountaineers.

OTHER COLLECTIONS
- Alan Rouse Memorial Library (Sheffield City Library)
- Fell and Rock Climbing Club Library (Lancaster University Library)
- Graham Brown Memorial Library (Scottish National Library, Edinburgh)
- Rucksack Club Library (Manchester Central Library)
- Scottish Mountaineering Club Library (SMC members only)
- Yorkshire Ramblers Club Library (Leeds Central Library)

AWARDING BODIES	
BODY	**OPERATION**
The International Federation of Mountain Guides Associations (IFMGA, or UIAGM in France)	Consists of National Guiding Associations of 17 member countries. All work to the same strict syllabus and assessment standards.
The British Association of Mountain Guides (BMG) or the American Mountain Guides Association (AMGA)	Train candidates for the IFMGA/UIAGM International Mountain Guides Carnet
The AMGA and Mountain Training UK (MTUK)	Set standards of training and assessment for instructor qualifications valid within US and UK, respectively

THE INTERNATIONAL GUIDES CARNET
(IFMGA GUIDE, USED TO BE UIAGM)

The highest award in mountaineering and climbing. It is the only internationally recognised professional qualification. Members are some of the most experienced and talented climbers and mountaineers in the world. In their home countries, qualified guides are members of their respective professional association, which trains and assesses members.

Becoming an IFMGA Guide is very difficult, with only several people each year making the grade. They are assessed in rock (E1), ice (grade 5), alpinism and skiing. They are also trained in a wide range of professional topics, including first aid and rescue training, sports physiology, coaching, the law, professional standards, environmental issues, mountain weather, snow science, avalanche forecasting, mountain history and flora and fauna.

The essential differences between the IFMGA Carnet and other qualifications are the greater level of experience and higher climbing standard required to start the scheme and the broader range of areas covered. You can be assured that anyone holding this award is seriously passionate about climbing. IFMGA Mountain Guides are widely respected for their quality of work, attention to detail and client safety.

MTUK AWARDS	
AWARD	**DESCRIPTION**
CWA	Supervising sessions on climbing walls, with an optional module for abseiling and climbing towers
SPA	A low-level award intended for leaders supervising groups top roping and bottom roping on single pitch rock climbs on crags and indoor walls. Although individuals may be highly experienced climbers, there is no way of knowing that from the award.
Walking Group Leader (WGL)	Leading groups in non-mountainous terrain, e.g. Dartmoor, England
Mountain Leader Summer/Winter	Holders of both of these awards are highly competent at leading walking trips in the UK in summer/winter conditions. It is not a climbing award.
International Mountain Leader (IML)	Leading walking groups in Europe in all areas, except on glaciers and where the techniques or materials of alpinism are required. Can also operate on easy, snow-covered terrain – including using snowshoes – providing it is of a gentle, Nordic type in the 'middle' mountains. In such cases, they will not spend consecutive nights outside, unless they use refuges with guardians.
Mountain Instructor Award (MIA)	The holder is trained and assessed to lead up to VS multi-pitch rock climbing and hill walking in summer conditions. Designed for the specific types of situations/conditions found in the UK.
Mountain Instructor Certificate (MIC)	The holder is trained and assessed as for MIA, but also at grade 3 for winter mountaineering and climbing. Designed for the specific situations found in the UK.

AMGA AWARDS

AWARD	DESCRIPTION
Top Rope Site Manager	Prepares climbers to safely teach top rope climbing and to manage group climbing sites
Rock Instructor Course	Introduces aspirant guides to multi-pitch guiding skills on rock routes up to grade III in length and with relatively simple approaches and descents
Advanced Rock Guide	Further prepares and evaluates guides on difficult terrain above grade III

GUIDING IN EUROPE AND THE ALPS

Strict laws apply to professional guiding in the Alps, with only IFMGA guides allowed to work legally in many countries with ice fall climbing and Via ferrata. If your instructor is working illegally, his insurance is likely to be invalid and so may yours!

CLIMBING EXPEDITIONS

There are few countries where laws apply to expedition guiding. To help differentiate professionally led expeditions from other trips, there is a new standard that guides may adhere to in order to use the IFMGA logo to advertise their expeditions. Any expedition meeting the IFMGA standard must be professionally planned, staffed by IFMGA guides and have thorough medical safety and evacuation contingencies, as well as radio and satellite communications at base camp and on the mountain.

MOUNTAIN WALKING AND TREKKING

This book is ideal for novices and experienced walkers alike, as it includes everything you need to know about how to navigate in the mountains. It includes information on weather, and tells you how to prepare for your trek, including packing your rucksack and the equipment you will require. It also demystifies the art of scrambling and tells you how to ascend Via ferrata safely.

ROCK CLIMBING

Rock climbing can be a tough, sometimes dangerous, physical and mental challenge. This book covers everything you need to know to be safe when ascending steep rock formations, including efficient movement skills.

ALPINISM

Venturing to the Alps for the first time can be daunting. This volume covers everything you need to know about ascending these magnificent mountains, in summer and winter.

SKI MOUNTAINEERING AND SNOWSHOEING

Mountaineering on skis or snowshoes requires the ability to ski off-piste, good navigation skills, and awareness of the risks of the mountain environment in winter – you will find all of the above and more covered in this handbook.

WINTER MOUNTAINEERING

Mountains transformed by snow and ice are a world apart from lush summer slopes. This volume provides you with the techniques to explore wintry plateaus, tackle rocky ridges and ascend snowy slopes.